THE SOUL OF YOUR PET

THE SOUL OF YOUR PET

Evidence for the Survival
of Animals After Death

Scott S. Smith

Illustrated with Photos

HOLMES PUBLISHING GROUP

The author would like to thank all those who contributed their time, photographs, and personal experiences. If you would like to contribute to the forthcoming sequel, see the last page of this book.

First Edition
1st Printing, 1998

ISBN 1-55818-408-2

Library of Congress 98-074077

The photographs illustrating this book were amateur shots and varied in age and quality, but every effort has been made to reproduce the images as clearly as possible.

For Nellie
1977-1997

For a Complete List of Publications,
Please address:
Holmes Publishing Group
Postal Box 623
Edmonds, WA 98020 USA

*"Who are we to say that animals don't have souls? Human beings
are just the most pompous things going!"*—Paul McCartney

According to *Pet Industry Magazine*, there are 70 million American
households with pets; a Gallup poll reported that a majority of these
regard their animals as members of the family. For many, it is an
emotionally wrenching experience when these beloved companions die,
something those who have never been close to an animal cannot
understand.

While belief in human immortality is strong, few people have more
than a vague hope their animals will survive beyond death, finding
little support in religion or science. In the early 1990s, I asked readers of
several magazines to send me experiences which might have a bearing
on this subject.

I was stunned by the response. Rather than "ghost stories" you could
dismiss as the result of overworked imaginations, the reports which came
in were amazing in their variety, complexity and credibility. Skeptics
who would be eager to debunk the encounters as the result of the wishful
thinking of grieving pet owners will be sorely disappointed. Experiences
were sometimes lengthy and multi-sensory, occurring to perfectly normal
people who usually did not have supernatural experiences of any kind.
One is left with the distinct impression that something very real if unusual
did occur and it is quite difficult to explain these experiences away.

Unless one is predisposed to do that, of course. It is one thing to maintain a healthy skepticism about the paranormal, to avoid being taken in by fraud or misperceptions. The late parapsychologist D. Scott Rogo, in 30 books about things psychic, took a hard-nosed approach in his investigations (he also gave me one of my first pet afterlife stories). At the same time, he did not make skepticism a religion and showed in *Psychic Breakthroughs Today* how extreme bias has blinded the likes of Carl Sagan, James Randi and their Committee for the Scientific Investigation of Claims of the Paranormal. Jeffrey Masson and Susan McCarthy, in *When Elephants Weep: The Emotional Lives of Animals*, explain why many scientists fear acknowledging animal personalities, even to the point of becoming highly unscientific in their attitudes in order to maintain that view. Then there are those with a religious agenda against acknowledging animal souls. Absolutely nothing will open the minds of debunkers; I believe objective people will find these initial reports impressive.

My own journey to accepting what is now obvious to me really began when I was 17. In 1967, I was reading one of the budding counterculture papers when I ran across an offer for literature about animal welfare and wrote away for it out of casual curiosity. Some weeks later I received graphic brochures about topics I had never thought about: vivisection, scientific experimentation on animals which often involved horrific torture for dubious gain, and just how that meat I so much loved got to the dinner table.

I went into a state of shock and a religious crisis. I decided that any faith which did not condemn cruelty to our fellow creation was false, making this an acid test issue in the search for truth. It was then that I also realized that while believing that animals had souls did not guarantee humane treatment, reverence for life was usually the result.

I went off to college, where I published an underground newspaper with a treatise on religion and animals; after a two-year stint as a missionary for my church in Germany, I returned to form a campus club, Reverence for Life, which eventually went national. I co-authored a book on the subject. I began a career in the natural food industry and later became an assistant to best-selling nutritionist Dr. Paavo Airola, in an effort to promote health not based on vivisection. I co-founded a vegetarian newspaper, then sold it to *Vegetarian Times* in 1978, where I served as associate editor till 1985. By then I was emotionally burned out with these crusades, discouraged by the juggernaut of cruelty.

I decided to take a break and do freelance investigative reporting on less soul-wrenching subjects, though the topics—Northern Ireland, the funeral industry—still often centered on death. Having grown up in a household where the afterlife was taken for granted, I found it puzzling that people feared death so much. I began reporting on the supernatural and learned just how credible reports about many paranormal phenomena were, and I realized the enormous implications of an unseen and eternal world swirling around us. As I read near-death experience literature, I was struck by the fact that no one mentioned encountering animals on the Other Side. In 1991, I began soliciting experiences from magazine readers.

As I talked and wrote about the accumulating evidence for animal immortality in the two years following my initial survey, more and more people would approach me with new stories. It became clear that there is a tremendous reservoir of experiences of this sort, that people are just now coming out of the closet about these things, as happened two decades ago with near-death experiences. The door has now been cracked open and there is obviously much left to learn (readers who have relevant experiences to report are invited to write the author c/o the publisher for consideration for possible future volumes on the subject).

Indeed, these experiences raise as many questions as they answer. Do animals go to some permanent heavenly realm after crossing the Great Divide or do they reincarnate? Do some or all have a group soul, merging back spiritually with their fellow creatures once dead, as some religions argue? Do they evolve spiritually into humans? Do pets survive because of their tie to humans or do wild beasts also have souls? What about insects? Where do you draw the line between plant and animal? Human and ancestral hominid? Why do some apparently come back to visit their former owners, while others do not? What is the point of so much seemingly needless animal suffering? The answer to these questions is that we need to first try to gather enough research to form a consensus that the animals about which we have the most information, pets, survive death at all. We need to get to first base before we speculate about matters about which we know even less (there are those who would delight in promoting discussing about whether cockroaches have souls, in order to ridicule discussion about whether dogs do).

Alas, the telling of the following tales naturally includes elements which are sad. It is not my intention to disturb those who are sensitive to the suffering of the innocent or who empathize strongly with the grief which pet owners feel in losing what are to them like little children. The final message, that human and animal members of families may be reunited, is, however, worth the expenditure.

This investigation would not have been possible without the support of those magazine editors who graciously allowed me to ask their readers to send in their experiences. I particularly appreciated the encouragement of Nancy Blanton at *Veterinary Forum* and Phyllis Galde of *Fate*, as well as the articles by Marigrace Heyer of the *Times News* of Lehighton, Pennsylvania. I also am indebted to Lew Regenstein and Tricia Lamb Feuerstein for help with research on religions. My wife, Vicki, was vital to the project, providing editing, research and encouragement motivated by spiritual and human values.

Finally, we all owe a great debt of gratitude to those who have shared their stories with this great message of hope. They are identified generally by state or province of last known residence in parentheses by the name and can be contacted via the author.

This report opens the door to one of the greatest mysteries and most important questions of all time, with implications we do not yet grasp.

CHAPTER ONE

A MEASURE OF OBJECTIVITY

Do animals have souls? Is there some essence of personality which transcends death for at least some beasts? Is it possible to meet a beloved pet again? For those who have never connected with an animal, it is difficult to understand that such companions are loved—and love—like little children. Their vulnerability and innocence make their suffering and death harder to take and the answer to the question as to whether they have an afterlife is one of great importance for those who care.

Given the fact that we are only the slightest fraction of life on this planet, it is a sign of our self-centered arrogance that we have never treated this question with much seriousness. Those who have had experiences with animals who seemed to return from death have often been afraid to mention them, lest they be considered crazy.

Yet, how can one decide whether to believe those who tell these tales of beastly immortality? Part of the credibility of the following experiences is that they cannot be easily dismissed as the result of the wishful thinking of grieving pet owners, the common assertion by skeptics. Those who would resort to complicated arguments to try to explain these away as hallucinations or misperceptions violate a central principle of philosophy, *Occam's Razor*. William of Occam, a 14th Century English thinker, enunciated the idea that the simplest explanation which accounts for all the facts is the one likely to be true. As each episode builds on those before it, one is left to conclude that these people are simply reporting a facet of reality, albeit one we have tried very hard not to recognize.

I have grouped the following experiences by the most important element which unites them and which makes each one seem likely to have happened as described. These categories are: no emotional attachment to the animal encountered (often the witness did not even know the animal once existed), lack of awareness that the animal was dead, multiple witnesses, and living pets reacting to an animal ghost (photographic evidence is also considered). Often the incidents include more than one of these validity markers. Of course, other elements of the stories may persuade one that the reports should be taken seriously, such as the hardheaded nature of the witness, the lack of other psychic experiences in the individual's life, and the fact that the pet which returned was not a favorite.

SIGNIFICANT OTHERS

In 1992, Dina Andrews, a veterinarian at the clinic where I took my own dogs in Thousand Oaks, California, was asked to go on a house call. An older white horse in Hidden Hills, a nearby wealthy suburb of Los Angeles, was colicking, an intestinal problem, and had been down all day. By the time she arrived it was dusk.

After treating the horse she provided the owners with follow-up instructions and suggested that they separate the ill animal from its companion, lest the other horse in the corral become infected from the fecal matter.

The owners looked at Dr. Andrews in bewilderment: they did not have another horse, they informed her. The vet looked back where she had seen another white horse, but it had disappeared. As she described it, however, the owners recognized the horse as one which had recently died. Perhaps, they suggested, it had returned to watch over its sick companion.

Dr. Andrews (Indiana), now a faculty member at the Purdue University School of Veterinary Medicine, obviously had no personal attachment to the deceased horse, an element of such experiences which I rank as the most important point in judging an anecdote to be believable. In addition, she had no idea that these people even had another horse or that it had passed away, so her independent witness is invaluable testimony in the search for evidence as to whether lower animals are more than temporary collections of matter with no lasting personalities.

Nor was this encounter the only one Dina Andrews had with someone else's departed animal. A friend whose dog had passed on had attached the collar to a key chain and left it in his truck. One day while she was riding in the truck she picked up the collar and immediately noticed that the dog was sitting on the floor on the passenger side. She asked her friend where his dog used to sit and he acknowledged that it was right where she saw the animal. "I saw the dog every time I got into the truck from then on," she recalls.

In 1993, Andrews visited her grandmother in California shortly after her grandmother's cat, Snucks, died. It was a difficult time, since the woman lived alone and had been very attached to the animal. "While I was there I twice saw Snucks, but I told my mother not to say anything, lest we upset my grammy. Of course, she did." Grammy's response, however, was that she already knew the cat was around.

Another uncanny horse experience happened to Eric Stealey (Florida). In the fall of 1973, he and his wife, Jackie, wanted to get away from the noise of the city for a rest. A friend, Allen, invited them to his sister's horse farm in northern Virginia. Becky had a few acres of pasture and a drafty old farmhouse with a barn where she boarded, trained and groomed horses.

"It was midnight by the time we arrived and the farm dogs barked as we drove through the gate," remembers Eric. "While Becky and Jackie had coffee in the kitchen and caught up on the news, Allen and I decided to stretch our legs by walking into the pasture, enjoying the clear night sky."

At first the horses shied away, then slowly came up to see if the men had any food for them. "We had stuffed our coat pockets full of apples and sugar cubes and they were not disappointed. They stood in a circle and took the treats we offered them. Gradually, most of the horses wandered away except for one which had stood away from the rest," he says.

It was a dark black stallion with a white star on its forehead. "It was very shy, but it seemed to want something to eat, too. I put the last apple on the ground between us and the horse and slowly it came forward and took it." Allen got closer and fed it some sugar cubes and soon was stroking its muzzle. They stood around smoking and talking for 15 minutes with the horse standing there. "We could feel the warmth of its flank and watched its breath shimmer in the moonlight," comments Eric. As they went back to the house, the horse followed, stopping at the beginning of the ring of light around the buildings.

They joined the women in the kitchen for a cup of coffee, after the cold night air. As they were turning in, Allen asked who owned the black stallion, and was told that there was none and none of the neighbors had one, either. Then Allen's sister realized that a horse fitting that description was killed by lightning on that spot a few months before and was buried near the barn.

"Neither Allen nor I pushed the point," Eric says. "The horse had really been there and was as tangible as any of us. There are those who would say that such a thing is not possible and is against the natural order of things. After that night, I know better."

This experience is made especially believable because it involved not only a lack of emotional attachment to the animal, but unawareness that the horse was dead, more than one witness, and extended physical contact (as investigators of psychic phenomena know, the other world can manifest itself physically in this one from time to time).

In addition, it should be noted that neither Eric nor Allen had any other similar experiences with other animals. Why would something like this only happen once? Melvin Morse, M.D., in his study of near-death experiences (NDEs), *Transformed by the Light*, shows a connection between NDEs, an increase in paranormal experiences among those who have undergone temporary death, and changes in the electromagnetic field of the body. Kenneth Ring, Ph.D., in *Heading Toward Omega*, believes NDEs and other experiences of the supernatural sort are tied to kundalini, a biological energy system which is theorized by much of Eastern mysticism. Other experiences or biological or environmental factors might trigger momentary electromagnetic changes or activation of kundalini. Perhaps the strength of the personality of the animal involved might have something to do with perception of its spirit. The fact is, paranormal experiences more often than not are one-time events, or they happen seemingly spontaneously. This makes them hard to assess scientifically, but they are none the less real.

Scott McKinney (North Carolina), a veterinary technician, by contrast has had multiple encounters with the spiritual essence of animals he has handled. In his first week as an animal clinic in 1983, he was called on to help with the euthanization of a Doberman pinscher. "He was a beautiful dog and I admit I cried, not for having to euthanize him, but for his release from pain. As we administered the formula, I was holding him and asking his spirit guide to take him back."

After the veterinarian left Scott to bag up the body to be put into the holding freezer, he looked over and "beheld the most beautiful sight: out of his body came a luminous haze. It clung to the body ever so slightly, then, in one snap, became a cloud over his old body. He bounced around the body for a minute and then slowly joined two more 'clouds' that appeared, before they all disappeared."

A year later, Scott convinced a woman that her terrier, who was dying of cancer, really needed to pass on, but was hanging on because of her attachment. She assented to euthanasia and spoke with the animal. Immediately, the dog made the transition. Just then he saw a shimmering come up from the body.

After a few years of training in shamanism, Scott found that his perceptions sharpened and he would sometimes see a flash of light leave the body as he bagged it after putting an animal down. A few times, he actually saw pets follow their owners. For example, in 1994, he helped with the euthanasia of a terrier mix. After the people left the room he saw the ghost dog go after them, no longer limping from arthritis as he had in this life. It was so real that he went into the other room to see what was there, which was nothing (why the perception did not continue is one of those unanswerable mysteries).

One day in 1988, the neighbor's German shepherd got into Lucy Zerr's yard (Pennsylvania), attacking her four kittens. She watched in horror as the dog grabbed one and in seconds it was dead. As it went limp, something white in the shape of a cat emerged from the body and then faded away. She was astonished because until then she had assumed that animals only had a "group soul," no individual spirit, temporarily drawing the spark of life from a merged consciousness of the same species. This underscores the point that people do not always witness something which conforms to their preconceptions, making hallucination unlikely.

As to why she could first see the spirit and then it became invisible, this is one of many paranormal issues no one is yet qualified to answer. One might also ask why some see spirits in definite form, others as cloudy images, as in Scott McKinney's initial encounter? Others see these things as if they are as solid as flesh and blood beasts. The argument that the mind influences the perception of the image would not seem to apply in Zerr's case, for one example, so we really don't know the answer. The premier parapsychologist, D. Scott Rogo, told me, just prior to his death, that after two decades of intensive research he was more at a loss for ultimate answers about the mysteries of the supernatural than ever.

In 1989, Denise Dmytrasz (California) was with her two sisters and mother in the parents' home as her father lay dying in the bedroom. As the family was talking at the kitchen table, Denise noticed some movement out of the corner of her eye. "I turned to look and saw a small dog walk past the doorway. I turned to my mom and asked when she got a dog."

Her mother told her they did not have a dog, so the family went looking through the house for the one Denise had seen. There was nothing. Later, they learned that the dog looked like the spitz her father had when he was young. "I believe the dog came to him to make it easier for the crossing over," says Denise.

She adds a significant comment: "I was surprised, because I never even knew my dad liked animals." In short, he was not one to fawn over a dog, at least as an adult, so no one would have imagined this event occurring.

While working in San Diego, California, in 1975, Mary Seiler (Nevada) had to go through the drafting department of her company one morning in order to make photocopies. It was well-lighted and full of people. As she passed by one drafting table, something caught her eye. "I looked down and to my surprise, I saw a gray cat with yellow eyes materialize. It leaped up and rubbed itself against the legs of the draftsman, who seemed oblivious, then disappeared," Mary says. "I was shocked! I was alert and observant and noticed that the cat seemed to lack depth, but had width and breadth."

She approached the draftsman and blurted out, "Do you own a cat?" He responded that he used to, but it had been run over two weeks before. He confirmed her description and thanked her for telling him, since he had felt the cat's presence many times, but thought he was imagining things.

Clearly, a busy drafting room with the witness preoccupied with routine business would hardly be the right environment and timing for to have hallucinated a ghost, especially of an animal. It stretches credibility to believe that Mary imagined this, then just happened to be lucky to ask someone who had lost a cat recently and have described it correctly? Skeptics, who cannot handle something like this actually having happened, can only fall back on one argument: this witness and many others are lying. Yet, she, like others, only claims to have had a single, short-lived experience a long time ago. Why not something more spectacular or frequent?

Rachel Arvio (Washington) was ten years old when her family lived on a very busy road where there were many accidents involving animals. "One day a large German shepherd was hit and I rushed out the front door to see what happened. The dog limped over to some myrtle under a tree and lay down. He made direct eye contact with me and stared very intently, then his eyes glassed over, almost as if a line were pulling up through his face. At that moment, I saw a cloudy white form leave his body."

Could she have fantasized such a thing, perhaps based on the family's belief in animal spirits? She answers this objection: "At that age, I had never heard of the etheric body and had no idea what I was witnessing." Nor did she ever see anything like this again, despite being at the scene of other accidents.

The famous psychic medium Eileen Garrett related a childhood experience growing up in Ireland in her 1949 book, *Adventures in the Supernormal*. When her parents committed suicide, she was given over to the care of an aunt. After being thrashed for claiming to see ghosts, she decided to exact her revenge by killing the aunt's favorite ducklings. As she did so, she was astonished to see a "blue smoke" arise from each one.

How does one explain this away? The child was too surprised to ignore this as merely the result of family tradition. This cannot be dismissed as an example of what skeptics of the paranormal would regard as Garrett's "psychic delusions," since this is essentially the same experience as that of Rachel Arvio, who has no such apparent abilities.

Another individual with paranormal abilities he labels "clairvoyant sensing" is M.T. Cunningham (Pennsylvania). In 1991, a young girl came to him for a reading. He kept getting impressions of a dog which looked like a German shepherd, which moved back and forth in front of the girl. "I joked that she must have a dog which needed to be let out of the house to go to the bathroom, but she denied owning a dog."

After the reading she asked some roundabout questions about the dog he had seen. When he described it, she said it fit the description of her dog who had died two months prior. The girl had felt she was in some way responsible for its death.

The girl could not see the dog, but a man who did not know she had a pet or that it had died gave her the message that life does not cease with death.

Another person with similar skills is Bevy Jaegers, who has assisted police around the country in numerous cases of murder and missing persons. She disowns the label psychic, says anyone can learn to do what she does, is very skeptical of most claims of supernatural experience and has the tough-mindedness of the cops she has worked with for so many years. Her modus operandi is psychometry, which involves touching an object and learning to see images which have been mysteriously attached to it during its lifetime. Although she cannot explain it, she is pragmatic and uses it effectively, just as an acupuncturist heals without being able to explain how his technique works to the satisfaction of mainstream medicine.

But while not one prone to "seeing things" outside her psychometric detective work, she did note a golden retriever lying by the door each time she visited a neighbor in St. Louis. When she finally commented on how beautiful it was, the neighbor was incredulous: the dog had died years before, yet Bevy described it accurately.

The family which had loved the dog did not see it, but a stranger could, who assumed it was alive. Bevy Jaegers has claimed to see no other ghost animals, so one cannot ascribe this incident to a tendency to see such things; nor is her police work similar to this experience, paranormal though it is.

Faye Ella Daugherty (Maryland) received a call one day from her sister-in-law, who lived around the corner, saying that her kitten had been killed in the street. "Later that day, I was coming out of the downstairs bathroom, when, lo and behold, there was her kitten strolling through the dining room doorway from the living room, walking five feet and disappearing under the table."

Her first impression was that her sister-in-law had been mistaken, that it was someone else's kitten who had been killed. She bent down to retrieve it and put it out, but there was no kitten there, nor anywhere else in the house. "This is the only time I have ever seen an animal that didn't exist!"

Frank Farnswarth (New York), now retired from a military career, had a golden retriever-collie male named Bobby for 11 years. The dog died in 1975. Then, in 1988, a friend was visiting his home when she said she saw Bobby leap from the living room couch and heard his clicking toenails on the floor. A few days later, Bobby's daughter who was named Bobbi, died at age 17. Frank believes that perhaps the father dog had come around to be with his daughter as she passed into the other world.

Frank also had a big gray and white cat. One day after it had been run over and killed, a young man who was a friend of Frank's daughter, dropped by the house for coffee. He was not aware the cat had died and commented on the "beautiful gray and white cat that ran under the table." Later, another friend saw the cat, but, knowing it was dead, was so scared that he stayed away from the home for six months.

Frank and his family, of course, did not see either pet. Any psychological or naturalistic theory as an alternative to acknowledging the spiritual nature of other animals has to take this into account.

Bobby (owner, Frank Farnswarth)

Frank's Portrait of the Animals that have been in his Life

Gail Parker (Pennsylvania), a member of the Dog Writers Association of America, had an Irish Setter, Rebel, now deceased, who provided silent testimony of another animal passing on. Gail had a rabbit named Bambi which she kept in a cage which had been made to resemble a piece of furniture. It was always in the house to avoid the harm which had come to other pet rabbits who were left in the yard. One day, two months after the rabbit passed away in 1986, Gail had cleaned the cage and was airing it. It was completely empty. Suddenly she heard the thumping which Bambi always made whenever he wanted attention. It was distinctive and not her imagination because Rebel also reacted. "I believe it was Bambi telling me 'I'm ok.'"

Bambi and Rebel (owner, Gail Parker)

Ellen Cutler (Michigan) says she has often encountered departed pets when visiting friends. Many she says she had never met in this life, but could accurately describe.

Often they would been seen walking across the room or in a favorite spot they had during life. But sometimes they had never even lived in that place. "I recently visited a friend's apartment, which she had lived in for a year, and saw the family dog, which had died 20 years ago. I never even knew she had a dog."

Some friends once had a female shepherd-collie mix named Sassy, Ellen says, and she grew to love "this exuberant and intuitive dog" during regular Friday evening visits. "When she was euthanized, I was not told where she was buried. Sassy continued to greet me on occasion at the door and one time I got the impression that she wanted me to follow her mentally. She showed me her grave and looked pleased when I understood. I confirmed the location and appearance with my friends."

Don Poston (Nebraska) recalled a German shepherd his father-in-law had, which died of old age. "One day I drove to his house. While I was stopped, I looked in the rearview mirror and saw the old dog walking away from the car. When I turned my head and looked back, it was no longer there, nor in the mirror."

Had Don imagined it? Then why did the image only appear just for a few seconds in the mirror, why did it not continue? Perhaps an element of perception flipped on which we do not yet understand, or a momentary rent in the cosmic veil between the worlds took place, or an electrical interaction between the dog and its environment. Maybe there was divine intervention to give him a story to pass on to others. The lack of answers does not negate the reality of the experience: he did not expect to see the dog, but did.

A Louisiana dog pound in Beauregard Parish developed a reputation for being haunted by ghostly hounds a few years ago. A veterinarian assigned to the shelter for night duty claimed he was regularly bitten by a German shepherd and other large dogs. The problem was that no such animals were at the pound at the time.

Then another vet on night duty was also attacked and he quit the next day. He described the animals as being similar to wolves, foaming at the mouth. Yet no dogs like that were there. Neighbors complained of constant howling and dogs running loose, even though when the police would arrive the place was quiet and all the animals were caged.

According to veterinary assistant Therese Faucher, they searched through department records and found dogs fitting the descriptions which had been in the pound the month before and had been destroyed. The shelter was closed because it was too difficult to get personnel to work there, due to its reputation.

How is it possible that a ghost dog could inflict a bite? Students of the supernatural know that this sort of intervention into the material from the unseen world is not uncommon. In this area, one can acknowledge a fact without understanding it.

In 1979, Clairyce Dolson (California) moved into a house for just 15 months. "The entire time I was there, I would catch glimpses of a black short-hair cat," she reports. "It would appear outside, lazing in a sunny spot or walking around the corner of the house; inside, it would walk from the sliding glass door to the kitchen or down the hallway." It was so real that she got up the courage to ask neighbors about it and was told the cat belonged to the previous occupants, but was hit by a car in front of the house shortly before they moved away. After she moved to another house nearby, she saw it a few more times in the flower bed of the other home as she drove by.

Joanne Grauer is a Los Angeles pianist who makes music tapes which she claims help to heal animals. "One evening I was performing at a supper club and a friend brought a group of people in to hear the music," she remembers. "As I was speaking with my friend, I noticed a small white dog with one eye sitting next to one lady in the booth. I told the woman what I saw and she began to cry. She had just lost her pet dog, Sugar, and this woman had been wondering if the animal was ok."

Joanne had never spoken to this person and had no previous knowledge about what the dog looked like.

Jane Blair (Tennessee) and her husband purchased an old farmhouse high in the hills. "On two occasions recently, I have seen a charcoal-colored cat, about half-grown, scampering across the living room floor, although it definitely is not alive."

24

Jane says there is "other paranormal activity" in the house and on the grounds. She speculates that the ghost cat hangs around to be with the living cats or because she likes people.

There does seem to be a disproportionate number of women reporting experiences with pets returning from the other side. Are women simply more attached to animals? Would that be enough of a magnet to draw in animals they never knew? Is the female brain attuned to realms the male is not? Or are women simply less afraid to admit to having these experiences?

The final anecdote for this category of testimony was reported by a young woman, but really happened to a male stranger. Regan Hallett (Arizona) now knows that animals which have passed on might communicate their afterlife in unusual ways. At Christmas of 1993, Regan was upset over the loss of her 16 year-old Siamese cat Scoobie Doo. "I didn't actually want to see her, since I'm chicken!" she laughs now. "I just kept saying to myself that I wanted some kind of sign that she was ok."

That night she had guests over. "When I went to the door, I was startled to meet someone named Kevin, who looked just like my friend Kevin Wieslander, who had been killed in a motorcycle accident a year before. As Scoobie Doo lay dying in my arms, I asked Kevin Wieslander to take her, since they knew each other."

Later that evening, with everyone relaxing and Christmas music playing in the background, this new Kevin leaned over and asked if Regan had a cat. She said yes, that Mr. Blue was in the backyard, since he was afraid of people.

"No, I mean a cat in the house," Kevin responded, "since I've been hearing a cat purr in my ear for the last five minutes."

The next day she asked the friend who had brought Kevin to the party if she had told him about Scoobie's death. She had not. "I'm convinced she's ok now, but I never would have imagined how I received my sign," comments Regan.

Judie Hurta (Wisconsin) went to visit a friend, Gayle. It was a hot day and Judie was thirsty. "I was told to help myself to ice water in the refrig," she remembers. "As I was getting a glass down, I noticed a white cat with brown spots uncurl itself from the floor by Gayle's feet and come walking over to me. I thought how pretty it was and asked Gayle when she had gotten the cat." She did think it odd, since Gayle's husband loathed cats of all types.

"I don't have a cat," Gayle replied. Judie looked down and as the cat started to rub against her it disappeared. Judie was so surprised she ended up pouring the water all over.

"I was there, I saw and felt it, and then it was gone, just like that," Judie recounts. "I couldn't see through it—it looked like a regular breathing feline." She described its markings to Gayle, who said her husband had shot and killed a wild cat like that the night before, burying it in the woods. It had been hanging around the mobile home and Judie feels that in life it was trying to get inside—which it finally did.

SURPRISED BY DEATH

Terry Rodefer (California) was working for the Los Angeles Parks and Recreation Department in the summer of 1977, building scenery for the teen summer theater program. One day while working on a prop at the work table, he became aware, out of the corner of his eye, of two black cats playing closely with each other. He turned to get a better look, but nothing was there. "I was sure they had not simply scampered out of sight. I would have seen that," he insists. "But I shrugged it off and went back to my work."

Soon they were back, in another area, and he caught glimpses to the side. Again, when he turned to look, they were gone. He made up his mind that the next time he would whip around his head so fast that he would not lose sight of them. But no matter how fast he turned, the cats disappeared.

"Three days later," Terry notes, "I received a letter from the couple renting my house in San Antonio, Texas, who were also in charge of sitting my cats, that a brother-sister pair of black cats were mysteriously 'gone': one was found dead in the yard with no indication as to cause, the other was never found. I believe that on their way to wherever, these two felines dropped by to say goodbye."

And, as Terry points out, "this is a case of an apparition in advance of my having any knowledge of the cats' demise, so that pretty much puts 'imagination' out of the picture." He also points out that the cats to whom he was most attached never appeared to him.

The experiences in this section have the predominant characteristic of an animal whose spirit was encountered before the witness knew the pet had passed over. Occam's razor suggests that the only sensible explanation is that this constitutes evidence for animal survival of death.

Nan Morowich (Georgia) was close to a collie-German shepherd called Beauty, who disappeared in 1977 when the dog was seven. One day a couple of months later, Nan looked out the kitchen door and saw the dog wagging her tail and acting happy, before vanishing. Three days later her niece's son came by to say he had found Beauty's body.

Nan says she frequently "sees things before they happen, but I don't like to talk about them because people look at me funny." She also had another experience of this sort with a black cat named Panda.

When Nan was 900 miles away one day she suddenly saw Panda, who was still at home, suddenly appear in her room crying "Ma, Ma" before disappearing. When she spoke with her brother by phone later, he told her the cat had died. Panda continued to appear to her afterwards, especially when it rained. "I could feel him walk around on the bed and then jump down and noisily walk around the floor," Nan adds.

"Especially when it rained"? Skeptics about the supernatural in general try to cast doubt on experiences by pointing to odd, unexplained and paradoxical elements. The net result is that they misuse reason to end up with an illogical conclusion. The question they refuse to answer in this case is, how could Nan have envisioned Panda's ghost just before knowing of her death? They will usually mumble that there probably is some explanation, we just don't know what it is.

Ruthie Falls (Burbank) frequently visited a friend who had many cats, some tossed into her yard by those who no longer wanted to care for them. Each time Ruthie was there, she would ask the names of each cat and her friend would tell her.

One night Ruthie dreamed that the deceased queen of the brood, Miss Purr, appeared to her, giving her name as if she could speak like a human. Next to her was a little gray kitten Ruthie had seen at her friend's house. The following day Ruthie called her friend to tell her about the dream and was told that the gray kitten had died that night. "She was so happy to know that Miss Purr was caring for her."

The odds of guessing correctly which of the numerous cats had died— if any—would be enormous. To argue that Ruthie Falls picked up the fact of the death telepathically would be to invoke a paranormal explanation which is no more "rational" in the view of skeptics than accepting the concept of a hereafter where the spirit continues.

One Friday night as Susan Baker (Maryland) was up late watching a movie on TV, as she would often do with her German shepherd, Baroness or Boo, she reached down to pat her, running her fingers through the hair on her neck. "Then I realized she was at the vet's, since she had been in much pain lately. "I looked down and there was Boo looking at me with her soft and loving eyes."

A whistle sounded from the other room and Susan and Boo looked up to see a man in blue, bent over in playful invitation to the dog. Boo sprang up and trotted through the doorway, pausing to look back at me and give a wag. The man hugged her and they faded away.

"The next day the vet called to tell me Boo had died in the night," claims Susan.

Susan Baker was also "forcibly adopted" by a black cat named Nam. "We were together during the university years, except the summers, which he spent with our friend Jane and her dog and cats. When I moved back home my father did not want a cat in the house, so until I could get my own place, Nam went back down to live with Jane."

A couple of months after the cat joined Jane, Susan awoke early one morning to hear meowing outside her window. "I looked out and saw Nam sitting on the ledge. I told him I would come and get him. I threw on a robe and went to the window from the outside, then pushed my way through the bushes. We 'hugged faces' and then he disappeared."

The next day, Jane informed Susan that Nam had died of pneumonia.

Viola Moulton (Florida) recalls an incident at the age of fourteen when she left her ill parakeet to attend a Campfire Girls camp. "During my first night there, really in the very early a.m., I was awakened by the gentle flapping of wings against my cheek," she says. "This continued for what seemed like several minutes and then ceased abruptly. I looked around the cabin for evidence of any birds and there was none. I was not frightened, rather, curious and puzzled."

When she called home, her mother told her that her parakeet had died in the night. And, it should be underscored, this was the only experience involving a deceased pet she ever had.

If birds might survive, what about fish? Hard though this may be to imagine, consider the case of Richard E. Lindahl, Jr. (Maine), who kept a couple of goldfish in his room. One night, he had a dream which was interrupted by the image of a goldfish floating in the air in front of him, slowly swimming away into the horizon. He woke up and checked the fish, finding one of them floating dead on top of the water. "I certainly had no idea it was even in poor health," Richard notes.

One could argue that he was simply "notified" about the death by some unknown force, his subconscious or some guardian entity. Certainly, someone or something regarded the death as important enough to send a message of some sort. Any satisfactory explanation involves the paranormal, and the image of swimming away would have been a good way to symbolize death and survival. Richard also notes that he had no great feeling for the fish, whereas he never had a dream or psychic experience involving his beloved and departed dog.

Lloyd Bannerman (Ontario), is a former professor of philosophy who taught courses entitled "Evaluation of the Occult" and "Loneliness, Despair and Death." He says he is "eclectically skeptical" and "almost completely insensitive to psychic phenomena." He is thus a good reminder that tough-minded individuals have these experiences as often as those who claim to have experienced other psychic phenomena. "My wife and I are also not the kind of people who like to cuddle or fondle animals," he adds.

They had no great emotional attachment to two cats, which their children left with them when they moved out. One day the 17 year-old calico fell ill and the Bannermans took it to the vet, who suggested they leave it overnight on a life-sustaining program and phone the next morning to discuss what to do with it.

"After going to sleep that night," relates Dr. Bannerman, "I suddenly awoke to an awareness of a sour smell which was associated with her illness. I thought that was interesting so I looked at the clock, which said it was one a.m., and went back to sleep. The next morning the vet phoned to tell us the cat had died in the night, probably around one a.m."

Peggy Little (Maine), now a manager of an oil service company, remembers the black kitten her family acquired while stationed in Spangdahlem, West Germany, in 1969. After an injury, it adopted a pattern of hiding and springing out, claws bared, attacking everyone in the house. They decided it had to go and found a German family who would take the cat.

A week after the cat was gone, Little was vacuuming and all of a sudden, the same cat sprang out! Stunned, she stopped and looked for it, but it had disappeared. But for the next two days she was plagued by these phantom attacks. Bewildered, she called the German family to be sure they still had it. They informed her that it had died about the time

30

of her first sighting. The cat kept popping into her view from time to time wherever she was, even after she left Germany.

Oddly, cats seek Peggy out when she visits friends, acting in an unusually friendly way, even though she does not count herself as a cat lover and is allergic to them.

One of the more unusual cases of paranormal advance notice of animal death occurred to friends of Dale Suess, an Oakland, California consultant for the funeral industry (human and animal). On March 11, 1994, Beau, a basset hound, died at 6:49 a.m. in Dale's arms. Ten minutes later, he called Lou and Dan, friends who had often taken care of Beau, to inform them of the dog's demise. Lou asked whether Beau had passed on 10 minutes earlier, which Dale confirmed.

At 6:49, Diddley, Lou and Dan's terrier mix, was sleeping in a corner while they watched TV. Suddenly he awoke and came over and sat in front of them. His face seemed to change into Beau's for a couple of seconds, then Diddley went back to his spot and laid down. Lou turned to Dan and said, "I think Beau's gone."

Now, if we were in charge of nature's laws, we probably would not have a manifestation of Beau occur this way: why not have the dog's ghost appear to Lou and Dan, or for that matter Dale? The fact is, whether we can explain the strange manner and timing of such occurrences, we would be in denial to pretend they do not happen.

Dale himself had two other experiences in which he suddenly knew that other companion canines, Tramp and his daughter Lady, had died, even though he was not near them. Any adequate explanation must involve the psychic world, and it is at least as likely as any other paranormal explanation that his pets notified Dale, a death-surviving mind contacting him after death.

Another unique incident involved the cocker spaniel of Sharon Damkaer (Washington). In late 1985, she called an elderly friend, Frances, in Texas who had done an extended pedigree (listing of a purebred animal's ancestors) of Sharon's first cocker, Muffin. The friend has to remain anonymous because she was very well-known and, though now herself on the Other Side, would not approve of her identity being known in this connection. Sharon told Frances that Muffin had died at the age of 16. Frances responded that she already knew that.

Frances had been compiling a lengthy history of cocker pedigrees so her work on Muffin (and another Damkaer dog) gave her information she could use in her other work. She published three volumes of this work before her death. "One evening as her own two cockers lay sleeping (she often worked into the wee hours), she saw a different blond cocker in her living room looking at her," Sharon recounts. "She said she thought it was my Muffin because she had seen photos of her. She had seen glimpses of this dog a few days before and felt it was because one of her own doggies was also named Muffin, and she reasoned that perhaps her frequent talking to her Muffin might have somehow summoned mine. That particular evening my Muffin seemed to be asking something of her and Frances thought Muffin was trying to tell her telepathically that she should try harder to trace Muffy's ancestors back to their earliest roots in England—something Frances knew I would appreciate because of my interest in one historic English cocker line in particular, the Obos."

Muffin (owner, Sharon Damkaer)

Frances felt compelled to cross the room and remove a book from the shelf. It fell open to a page that mentioned a dog which she knew was in Muffin's pedigree and which was probably the link she had been hoping for to trace the line to England. Frances put aside her other work and spent several hours working on that line, confirming the connection.

"I found comfort in this story all these years," comments Sharon, "because I had no contact from my beloved Muffy myself after her death, but I thought she would have known I would be happy to find that her line went back to the Obo cockers." Sharon adds that she is not a religious person, but has had two experiences involving human spirits, so does believe in life after life. If one is to say that a psychic disposition explains encounters with ghost pets, why would Sharon have human but not animal contact?

Deems and Pat Peterson (Kansas) were looking for a house to buy in 1970. They found one they liked and visited a number of times before making an offer. Each time they visited the house the family dog was lying at the foot of the bed in the master bedroom. "It seemed to be 'his place' in the house," comments Deems.

They bought the house and put their bed in the same location as the previous owner. "About a year later, my wife got up in the middle of the night to go to the kitchen," Deems recalls. "I stayed in bed. All the lights were out when she returned to the bedroom. As she entered the doorway, she let out a scream and turned on the light. At this point I looked up and saw a misty gray vapor rise from the foot of the bed. Standing in the doorway, she saw exactly the same thing for a couple of seconds from a different vantage point."

The Petersons did not understand what it could be until a few days later when neighbors mentioned that the dog who used to live there had just died. "It seems to us that the dog probably returned to where he had lived for many happy years."

Like many of these experiences, this involves more than one category:

a case of an apparent ghost encounter without knowledge of the death of the animal, strengthened by being witnessed by more than one person. Why would two people imagine the same thing in the same place at the identical time, seeing an animal they did not know who had just passed away? It is hard to think of a reasonable explanation that does not involve the supernatural. But skeptics often are so wedded to a materialistic bias they will accept any absurd theory rather than stretch their acceptance of the very limited universe they insist they understand completely.

MULTIPLE WITNESSES

The next strongest category of evidence about animals surviving death would be those involving multiple witnesses. One individual's testimony might be ignored; it is harder to argue that more than one had a common misperception.

Karen McInnis (New Mexico), now a veterinary assistant to her husband, relates a remarkable multiple-witness story which took place in the early 1960s when she was a child. Their black-spots-on-white English setter, Pete, had to be euthanized because he was very ill. Shortly thereafter they moved from Alpena to Bay City, Michigan.

One winter day, one of the younger brothers, Peter, age eight, was found sitting by a heating vent and Karen asked him why he wasn't sitting right on top to get the maximum warmth. "Because Pete is lying on the vent," he responded matter of factly. He knew the dog was dead, but it was there anyway and he accepted it. Others in the family were not surprised and admitted having also seen the dog's ghost around the new house.

Karen herself did not see Pete until the following summer, when one day she was standing in the kitchen with her mother and the dog appeared at the back door, lumbered through the kitchen past her father, who moved out of the way, and lay down on the vent, which now brought in cool air.

In addition to Karen, her parents, two younger sisters and an older brother, other witnesses were added over the years. One was a sister who was not born at the time of the ghost's first appearance. She began toddling towards the back door one day, then suddenly stopped short and started crying "doggy, doggy, doggy." Then there was the friend of Karen's brother who dropped by and commented that he didn't know the family had a dog. After he described the setter, the family explained that the dog was really a ghost. He thought they were crazy. Eventually, the family adopted another dog and from that time onwards the old setter stopped appearing.

Those who believe that spirits are just mysterious imprints on the environment where the living being used to roam would be hard-pressed to apply this theory to this situation, in which the departed pet only started appearing after the family moved to a new location. To argue that perhaps they were all projecting this on the new environment invokes an explanation no less paranormal and more complicated—because it requires ascribing great power and motivation to the minds of many people, some not family members—than using Occam's razor to accept the spiritual nature of beasts.

Kathy West (Washington), a veterinary assistant, tells a tale with a similar ending. When she was 18, her cat Theodore, passed away. "That night I went to bed and around 3:00 a.m. I was awakened by a noise outside my bedroom wall, which is how Theodore always woke me up when he wanted in the house in the middle of the night. As I started down the stairs out of habit, I realized he was dead and the noise suddenly stopped." Her dog, Buffy, also seemed to notice the scratching and got up with Kathy at the same time. (See the next section with regard to animal witnesses.)

Several days later her mother mentioned that she had heard Theodore in the garage in the middle of the night, and not once, but several times. The same day, her younger brother told them that Theodore had been sleeping on his bed that night. He woke up to see the cat jump off his bed and go down the hall. Her brother followed him and when the cat reached the stairs he disappeared.

"We decided that Theodore was trying to tell us something, so we decided to get another cat. We sent to the Humane Society that day and picked out a kitten. Theodore didn't return after that."

In June 1994, Kathy received a call at the veterinary hospital where she works. Priscilla Speicher (Washington) said she, her husband, Bob, and daughters, Jamie and Suzy, who had just had their cat, Minky, put to sleep due to cancer, were upset because Minky seemed to still be in the house. The kids were afraid to go into their room. Each of them had, on different occasions and in different parts of the house, heard the cat's distinctive meow. Kathy advised that the cat must have something to finish before she passed over or perhaps she wanted the family to get another cat "to take care of them." They did get another cat and Minky did not return.

Minky (owner, Kathy West)

Roxanne Morgan (California) had a beautiful golden labrador which aged rapidly after 10 years. When the dog became incontinent, they made up a bed in the garage and she would bark to be let out in the morning. One morning after she was walked, the dog went directly to bed, unlike her normal tendency to stay up with whomever was home. The next morning, Roxanne heard her bark and when she went to let the dog out, found her dead. The veterinarian said that she had to have died about the time she went to the garage the prior evening.

Could the vet have been mistaken or could Roxanne have imagined the bark out of habit? For weeks afterwards, family members claimed to feel the dog's presence and catch glimpses of her.

World-famous psychic Averi Torres of Malibu, California, had a schnoodle (schnauzer-poodle mix) named Sunny for 15 years who had an uncanny ability to read her mistress's mind and was sensitive to the feelings of people in general.

"Just after Sunny died, I was conducting a women's group which Sunny liked to attend," Averi recounts. "She was usually well-behaved, but had a weakness for chocolate chip cookies and would wait until we closed our eyes for meditation to steal the refreshments. This time we were conducting a ceremony for Sunny's entry into the next world when they noticed that a piece of cookie was being lifted off the plate by something invisible!" Later in the meeting, one of the women felt something jump into her lap, just as Sunny had done while she was living.

Lawrence Bond (Washington) relates an experience he had as a boy. "We had a white terrier named Pinky we believed was poisoned by a neighbor. After she died I saw her occasionally run from a little shed in the back of the yard to the doggy door that led to the back of the house and porch. Then she would disappear."

He thought he was fantasizing it until his mother told him she had seen the same thing. She added that the dog would look up at her and show its teeth, something he did not see the dog do. Interaction suggests this was not an "imprint on the environment" and it seems unlikely that mother and son would hallucinate the dog taking the same path, ending up with the animal disappearing.

Sheba was a six-year-old timber wolf trained for sledding in the late 1970s. She was given to the father of Annie Boswell (Massachusetts) as a guard dog because a friend thought she was vicious. "I was told to stay away from her, but she looked so happy when I petted her and she was very affectionate. I took her off the chain so we could play." She was later shot by hunters who mistook her for a wild dog.

"One night I woke up to find her curled up at the foot of my bed as she always had done," Annie remembers. "I thought it was a dream until my mother and brothers also said they had seen her."

Vivianne Creelman (Connecticut), had a Maltese named Noel, which died suddenly. Shortly thereafter, she would catch glimpses of the dog, but said nothing to her daughter, Robin, for about two years, since Robin seemed fearful of the supernatural. "Finally, we saw Noel together and I told her about my previous experiences. She admitted to having seen her several times before, as well."

Devi Redfield (California) paid a visit to her grandmother's house in the spring of 1974. "As I reached for the screen door handle, I saw a black and tan dog staring at me through the door," she says. "He was wagging his tail a little, then turned and ran down the long entry way. Then I realized that my grandmother did not have a dog."

Later at the family gathering, an aunt told her that she and another aunt and the grandmother had also seen the dog, each at different times within the previous year. Twice he had been seen running across the flower bed and through a solid door. He did not resemble any pets that Devi's grandmother had ever had (hence, no one can explain these sightings as the result of personal emotional attachment).

The ghost dog seems to appear when unfamiliar people have visited the house, as if "checking out" the guests, notes Devi. "Six people to date have seen the dog. All agree as to its appearance—two feet high, black body with tan eyebrows and paws, short ears, curly monkey-type tail, large, dark eyes."

Devi Redfield also adds this significant point: "For just one second when I saw the dog through the screen door, I remember an alteration of my surroundings, with everything having a slightly hazy iridescence." This could be taken as an altered state of consciousness common to paranormal experience. If the argument is that this represents a sign of impending hallucination, that would mean that all the witnesses at different times went into the same state and saw the identical dog. If we were making an argument that complicated in favor of some supernatural theory, the skeptics would be amused at how far we had to bend the facts to fit our theory.

Linda Ospalski (Illinois) recalls her experience with a cat as a young woman some 20 years ago. Mickey was the last of her grandfather's cats and used to roam all day. One evening he returned full of scratches and Linda decided not to let him wander anymore. Later, she found him trying to use the litter pan without success and she rushed him to the vet, who said to leave him overnight for surgery for a bladder blockage. Linda figured she would bring him home the next day. That night she received a call letting her know that Mickey had died on the operating table. She felt bad that she had never had a chance to say goodbye.

A few days later, she began to hear a cat crying outside the back door, where Mickey used to come in from his wanderings, a cry just like his. "I kept hearing this in the evening for a week. I would open the door and nothing was there. One evening my aunt came over and we were sitting in the kitchen when the crying started. She heard it, too, and I told her about Mickey. She suggested I open the door and let him know that he is welcome to come in and that I knew he was all right. I did that and ever since that day, I have never heard the crying again."

Even if we assume that Linda imagined Mickey coming back from the dead because she wanted to say goodbye, how do we account for the aunt? The theme of pets returning to let their owners know they are fine comes up over and over, suggesting intelligence, survival and perhaps divine intervention.

I. L. Heiberg (Wisconsin) has a vivid recollection of Trusty, a German shepherd his family had for 14 years. "She was a clever dog who used to creep into my bed very stealthily, putting one paw in it to see if I would wake up and object, then another, until she was lying across my feet," he recalls. She was also unusual in that she loved the water and would go swimming on her own. "I never realized that animals have feelings until one day we were playing tag with Trusty and as she tried to avoid my brother and me she leaped into the air and tried to make a circle, but missed and fell on her side. She looked so clumsy we laughed at her and she crept away, tail between her legs and ears down. We immediately realized our mistake and went and hugged her until she seemed to feel better, but the fun had been taken out of our day."

It was with great sadness that the Heiberg family was forced to euthanize Trusty when they moved to Portland in 1941. During the spring of 1945, they decided to visit the old home. "I was sitting in dad's Dodge pick-up truck waiting for him to come out when I looked out the side window and there was Trusty, as plain as could be, with her tail wagging and her front feet on the truck running board looking up at me with a big doggy welcoming grin on her face." He thought he was going out of his mind, so he looked ahead through the windshield and then back again, but Trusty was still there. He did it again, finally getting out of the truck to tell his mother what happened.

When he did, he found out that his brother had also seen the dog when he stepped out the back door. "She had bounded towards him with a happy grin on her face, tail wagging. She was also transparent, he said, and he turned and ran to the house." His brother at first told his mother to keep the sighting a secret, afraid his brother would think he was crazy. "I was 31 at the time and my brother was 29, so we were old enough to be certain of what we saw," I.L. asserts now.

Ten-year-old twins Hans and Herbert Willner of Hamburg, Germany, were swimming in Lake Constance near the Austrian border when they began to have difficulty way out in the icy water more than 30 feet deep. As they started to flounder, the father, Dietrich, began to out in the lake after them.

Suddenly, in front of a dozen eyewitnesses, the family's beloved collie, Fritz, which had been dead for nearly a year, appeared by the boys. "He brought them all the way to the beach and dropped them off," Dietrich stated at the time. "While we were tending to them he just disappeared— he didn't run off, he just disappeared." The police report confirms this.

If all involved hallucinated, how were the boys rescued? They knew the dog too well to mistake it for another, and its disappearance belies any natural explanation. Skeptics may feel confident ignoring a few eyewitness reports, but as they mount up, their position that nothing like this could possibly occur becomes essentially a "religious" dogma which flies in the face of all the evidence.

Betty Smith (Manitoba) had a poodle-terrier named CoCo. A couple of days after the dog had to be put down after a poisoned ham bone was thrown in the yard, Betty saw CoCo curled up in her favorite chair. "She looked at me and then just disappeared. It was very clear."

Her mother, who lived in the same house at the time, also saw the dog running around her bed and then felt the dog curl up behind her exactly where CoCo slept when the family was away, although her hand could feel nothing.

Later, Betty went over to her sister's home across the street. A friend of her sister's who was visiting asked where Betty's dog was. "I explained that I no longer had a dog, but she insisted that she had seen one fitting CoCo's description following me across the street. She had never seen CoCo while she was alive."

Twenty years ago, Don and Julie Poston (Nebraska) acquired a German shepherd puppy, which they named Carla. She was very sick and whenever they would go downstairs to do the laundry the dog would cry at the head of the stairs until one of them would bring her down.

Ten years after her death, something odd happened, says Don. "My wife was standing in the bathroom doorway and I was in the hall at the head of the stairs. We were facing each other, when suddenly at the head of the hall we saw our Carla materialize. She ran past us to the head of the stairs and ran up them. This happened very fast." They looked at each other in astonishment, saying simultaneously, "Did you see what I saw?" They decided that Carla was trying to convey that she could now manage the steps and was doing well in the hereafter.

Even if we concede that both might have subconsciously desired to see their dog again, can we seriously believe that they would have imagined Carla's appearance at precisely the same moment?

Lee Gandee (South Carolina), mentioned previously, wrote about supernatural animals in *Strange Animals*, experiences he further detailed in letters. When he was 12, someone gave the family a spotted short-haired terrier puppy, whom they named Trixie. His mother's foster father, Hilary Hively, an agnostic, lived with them prior to his death in 1935, when Lee was 18.

"Trixie was inconsolable and would not eat for days, insisting on lying on a chair by his bedside as she had during his illness," recalls Lee. "Sometimes she would raise her head, make licking motions and wag her tail, as she often did when he used to reach out to her. She would also get up and go to the rocker in the living room, just as she would when grandfather would slowly stagger there." The family also heard shuffling steps around the dog.

"Trixie slept in a bed right outside my window," continues Lee. "She had the habit of snoring as loudly as a person and I would have to get up and turn her over to get her to stop." One night it sounded as if she were choking, but before the boy could get up, she stopped. He supposed she had changed her position herself, but the next morning he learned that Trixie had passed on. He made a little casket and buried the dog.

A week later, the family was at breakfast when they heard Trixie barking in the dining room and her toenails clicking on the linoleum as she ran to the front door. "Go see who it is at the door so early," said Lee's mother, but he reminded her that there was no longer a dog to bark at someone coming to the front door. "Oh, dear Lord," she replied. But the family could hear what seemed to be Mr. Hively's shuffling in the house.

One day, a neighbor dropped by. "I'm glad you got a new dog," she commented. The family denied it but the neighbor told them that it was barking when she was knocking on the door. They were forced to tell her what was going on and tales of their haunted house soon got around the neighborhood.

One night while he was cramming for an algebra exam, completely absorbed in trying to master it, Lee gradually became aware of snoring outside his window. It sounded like Trixie and he ran and got his grandmother, who could also hear it. They decided that neither Trixie nor Mr. Hively realized they were dead, so they sent for a local spiritualist to get advice. He told them that the next time they heard the supernatural sounds to just explain that their presence was distressing and it was time to move on to the next world. "That's what we did and we never heard the ghosts of grandfather or Trixie after that.

REACTIONS OF LIVING ANIMALS

The bulk of the evidence in the Gandee family tale above is of the multiple witness sort. But Lee does add one twist: they got a new dog, Zippy, while the ghost of Trixie was still around, and Zippy seemed to run in fright whenever Trixie's toenail clicking would come into the room. This sort of experience gives us a different kind of tool to assess the reality of stories of ghost pets.

The final two categories of evidence for which one can provide the most verification and which are the most difficult to easily dismiss differ from the ones above. Depending on one's point of view, they are the weakest or the strongest types of evidence of this sort.

If critics believe that witnesses are imagining these things, how do they explain the following examples, in which living pets reacted to ghost animals? I regard these as actually the strongest form of evidence of the external reality of reported encounters with the animal dead. These experiences as related are often brief because one cannot ask the animal witnesses for more details, but they require skeptics to go through more intellectually dishonest contortions to avoid drawing the conclusions which naturally follow.

Categorization can be complicated and sometimes I put more weight on the predominant character of a story, rather than what I think is theoretically the most important point in my hierarchy of validity. The question always is, what is the most important factor making this believable? For example, Kathy West's multiple witness case cited previously mentions in passing that her dog seemed to respond to the ghostly scratching, but that struck me as paling against the details reported by the human witnesses. In the following experience, we have vague reference to several human witnesses, some strangers to the animal, but no details, so the multiple responses by a living pet stands out and it fits better here, rather than under the multiple witness category.

Jill Hoff (California) reported that not only did she, her daughter and other people who visited their house see a departed Siamese named Sam walking around, but so did their young cat Abby. "From time to time, she would be lying or sitting quietly and suddenly would jump up and hiss at the spot where Sam used to sit, fur raised, and then run to my bedroom." (This was written some time ago and we have since lost contact, depriving us of further information).

A similar incident is related by Suzanne Kane, who runs a Fillmore, California, abandoned pet placement service, the Human Animal Rescue Team and edits the well-known "Muttmatchers" newspaper. One of her own dogs, Connie, a chow mix, had a favorite place to lie down on the hearth, she says. One evening after Connie had passed away, a friend brought over another dog named Coco. Coco decided that the fireplace looked like a comfortable place and proceeded to lie down right on Connie's spot. Suddenly, the fur flew. "Coco appeared to be in a wild fight with something invisible and never approached that spot again," Suzanne says.

Experiences with some commonality to those stories are related by "Juanita Martinez" (New Mexico), a registered nurse with a Master's degree, which ought to give her some credibility, but she has adopted this pseudonym and changed the name of her pets in the story because in her area this tale would be evidence of "brujeria" (witchcraft).

Juanita acquired Viki when the dog was just five weeks old. They used to take walks together for the 18 years Viki was alive. And they seemingly did so even after the dog passed on, for other dogs would bark at Juanita and then stop, seem to touch noses with an unseen dog at her side and then circle the presence, much as they did when Viki was alive.

Soon after Viki passed on Juanita had to move to another town 200 miles away. In the moving truck she was driving she felt something curl up on her lap, just as Viki always did. Her cat Fluffy sat beside her and would lean over, apparently touching her nose to something on her mistress's lap, just as she did when Viki was curled up there. When Juanita felt the weight move off her lap, Fluffy would climb on, trading places several times during the trip (Fluffy did not try to get on Juanita's lap as long as the invisible weight was there).

Betty Smith (Manitoba) believes her elkhounds, Tracy and Holly, had an encounter with her late poodle-terrier, CoCo. "One day, Holly started chasing 'nothing' down the hall into my bedroom, then back down the hall. She ended up on my bed, standing in the position she takes when she is 'daring' another dog. She was looking right at CoCo's favorite spot. Tracy also barked at the 'thing'."

The argument that Betty was just misinterpreting imaginative play might fly, except for the multiple human witnesses of Coco's ghost, as related earlier.

CoCo (owner, Betty Smith)

John Watts (Florida) also had an experience of this order. He had several dogs, one named Mr. Peke. The others learned not to disturb Mr. Peke when he lay in his favorite spot by the fireplace. However, they would walk across the spot if he were somewhere else. "After Mr. Peke died, the dogs would come to that spot and at certain times would walk through it, but at others they would walk around it, acting as if Mr. Peke were there."

Lee Gandee (South Carolina) was born in 1917 in West Virginia and is a retired state research analyst in real property who describes himself as a "Taoist-Christian freethinker." As a young man, he got a second dog, Zippy, after his Trixie passed on (a story we will tell later). "After Trixie died we would hear toenails clicking on the linoleum floor. Zippy's hair would bristle as he would edge past Trixie's favorite haunts, such as her bed on the porch and the place she liked to lie in the living room."

If one argues that Zippy was just avoiding Trixie's scent, why the bristling? Why not react to the smell in other parts of the house? With nothing physically there, such a strong reaction over and over to a very slight remaining smell would seem unlikely, especially after the first sensing. Buying into that explanation would also mean that it was wholly coincidental that a number of people heard what sounded like Trixie walking across the floor during the same period.

Paul Wiener (California), a technical writer now in the Los Angeles area, was living with a friend in the late 1960s in New York City. She had a malamute mix, one-eighth timber wolf. Paul had an ambivalent relationship with the animal, which had a vicious streak and would attack other animals and people. The bites Paul received were, however, considerably less serious than those inflicted on others and most of the time Paul and the dog got along well. Eventually, however, it had to be put to sleep because of its behavior.

For several years thereafter, Paul found that even dogs he had been friendly with for years would shy away from him, sniffing at something invisible by his side and backing off as if afraid. This can't be explained by remaining scent. Again, we have different people and animals at different places and times, yet similar experiences: the animals clearly sensing something the humans couldn't see. The only real puzzle is why the malamute would have preferred to hang around Paul rather than his mistress.

In 1984, Dee Dee Mascetti, a Burbank, California, self-described psychic, had to put her cat, Shrimpie, to sleep at age 18. One evening a year later, her other cats, Guy and PJ, were sleeping on the couch next to her as she watched TV.

"I looked over and saw Shrimpie exiting the kitchen. Guy and PJ both sat up suddenly and, with hair standing on end, watched intently as Shrimpie walked along the wall of the living room to the second bedroom. As we watched, Shrimpie walked through the enclosed door of the second bedroom." Guy and PJ ran to the door to sniff, but when Dee Dee opened it the two cats "ran like hell in the other direction and it took them a while before they would enter that room again."

Shrimpie made appearances for three years, no longer returning because, Dee Dee feels, Shrimpie sensed her mistress had been sufficiently

47

comforted about the cat's continued existence. But another cat from the Other Side has recently been visiting.

Dee Dee has seen a long-haired white cat twice inside her house and once outside, a cat which does not belong to anyone in her area and could not get into her house in any event. She believes it is the departed pet of a former owner. Her two current cats react strongly to this phantom, the younger one, Candy, fleeing in apparent fear each time the white cat makes its sudden appearance.

Renee Alvarado (Texas) was living in West Germany in 1965, sharing a room with her sister. Their dog was a short-hair spitz with black eyes named Spitzy. She slept at the foot of Renee's bed.

One night Renee awoke to Spitzy's growling. "She was on top of the bed looking down, where there was an exact replica of my dog standing there. The eyes were coal black, glowing incredibly, and I got an excellent look because the hall light made it easy. I remember it like it was yesterday. The hair was not distinct, rather a soft but solid outline."

She was so terrified that she could not get a word out. The strange dog ran towards the hall and disappeared. Renee wonders if perhaps the ghost was that of Spitzy's mother.

Mary Peed (Georgia), now retired from a career as an elementary school teacher, attributed her children's claims of poltergeist activity in their home to overactive imaginations, until things began to happen to her. One matter involved her beloved gray poodle, Tiffany. As the dog became blind, the other animals in the household, a Siamese cat and a German shepherd, became more attentive to her, keeping her from falling in holes and playing gently with her. At 14, Tiffany finally passed on and the other pets seemed despondent for days. Mary vowed not to get another animal. Being ill and house-bound herself, however, she eventually opened her heart to her daughter's Christmas present, a Pomeranian pup she named Foxy.

"Quite often I have noticed that Foxy stands on the edge of the bed and stares down intently, as if watching something enter the room,"

Mary says, "following it along the edge of the bed and around the chair. For a long time I wondered what he was seeing. Then one night I caught a glimpse of Tiffany walking into my room. I have also seen her shadow scampering about." This supports the likelihood that when animals seem to be encountering ghost pets, they probably are, even when their owners can't see anything.

Sandy Mauck (Illinois), now a psychotherapist, says that in 1968 when she and her husband were living in Huntington Beach, California, they were near a highway where pets were frequently struck by cars. It was thus foreboding when one of their short-haired domestic cats, Sugar, disappeared, although they never found the body.

"One day some time later, I was sitting in the apartment when I saw Sugar race up the stairs with her living litter mate, Spice, right behind. Sugar went right through the back door, which was closed. Spice stopped short, surprised to find his playmate was no longer there."

This involves something which cannot be explained as a simple illusion or reflection, since Spice was following the spirit cat closely for more than a moment, and both human and animal witness clearly were reacting to the same thing when the ghost went through the door.

Mary Ann Hirzi (Wisconsin) tells two hair-raising stories of supernatural brutes seen by both humans and pets. In November 1990, her sister was visiting and as they talked in Mary Ann's dining room, the sister said she saw the recliner in the living room open up and a humped black form "like an armadillo" sprang behind the couch. They went in looking for it, finding nothing. Was it the sister's imagination? Unlikely: several cats in the room were staring in the direction of where the ghost beast disappeared, hair on end, paralyzed by fear. One of her dogs came into the room and began sniffing the couch area intensely. Her sister was so frightened she left immediately.

A month later, Mary Ann was getting ready for bed when she saw her orange cat streak across the hall into another room. Right behind it came something that looked like a large dog with a pig's face and hooves.

It glanced at her and followed the cat into the other room. Mary was scared to death, but, after futile calls to her orange cat, went into the neighboring room. Her cat stood there, back to the wall, tail arched, eyes wide, frozen like a statue. There was nothing else in the room. From that point on, the cat, who had previously favored hiding under beds, never went under any bed again. Weird though this tale is, if one assumes both encounters were with the same beast, there were multiple human and animal witnesses.

"Sam came into our lives by walking up the driveway in 1960," remembers Roseanne Graff (Michigan) about her dog. "Whenever he would come home, he would walk under my hand as a greeting, his thick curly hair brushing my palm."

In 1967, the third day after Sam's death (which accords with ancient belief about how long the soul stays near the body), Roseanne was sitting on her couch daydreaming. She felt Sam's usual brush under her hand and thought, "Oh, Sam's home," then realized that was impossible. "I looked over and saw him walking out the door." We have two senses confirming the experience, but the next element of the story is the most important.

As Roseanne watched him walk down the driveway, Alfie, their wolfhound, threw back his head as Sam's ghost came by and let out a mournful howl, something he had never done and never repeated. Although this incident stretches our conception of reality, it is preposterous to believe that it was entirely coincidental that Alfie's singular howl happened just as Roseanne saw Sam walk by.

Vivianne Creelman (Connecticut) has a number of Maltese dogs and there is simply not enough room for all of them on the bed, where they would like to sleep. They trade off sleeping in the kitchen at the other end of the hall from her bedroom, with a baby gate blocking the way. However, sometimes one of them will manage to get around it and when it does, she can hear the dog running down the hall to her bedroom.

"One night I heard the steps coming towards us and the dogs on the bed and I watched to see who would come through the doorway," remembers Vivianne." Needless to say, we were surprised to see a white Maltese named Noel, who had died recently. He ran to the side of the bed, with the three dogs lined up on the bed watching him. He must have disappeared under the bed because one of the dogs jumped down and looked underneath. So did I, hanging upside down, but there was nothing there. They kept looking for Noel and it took several minutes for them to settle down."

Four witnesses, two senses, only one sensible explanation. But even very intelligent people can resort to theories with obvious holes in them when they are desperate to ignore the implications of the facts.

"I have had countless cats," says Olga Newman Adler (Connecticut), a retired artist and designer. "A Himalayan, named Bogar (bug in Hungarian), and a tortoise-shell, Csibe (meaning chicken—she was as tiny as a mouse and chirped like a chicken when we found her) had a favorite game, which was to run back and forth and jump over each other." While Olga was in the hospital in 1987, Bogar died of kidney failure. "When I came home I saw his shadow darting around on the floor and this happened from time to time. Whenever the shadow appeared, Csibe would sit up and stare, ears perked up and eyes wide, then begin running back and forth, leaping into the air at intervals much the same as she had done with Bogar when he was alive and her playmate."

Why would a ghost cast a shadow? This is unusual and our ignorance about the true nature of the universe is once again confirmed.

PHOTOGRAPHS

The final type of evidence where we have the most theoretical opportunity to check its validity involves photographs. Careful analysis of photos can often expose them as fakes, but sophisticated methods could make detection extremely difficult (and expensive). Natural elements and technical flaws could lead one to imagine a form not really there. The most one can say about the following cases is that the individuals who took the pictures seemed to have integrity and fraud seems unlikely. In some cases, there is some additional support for the validity of the photos because of timing of related experiences.

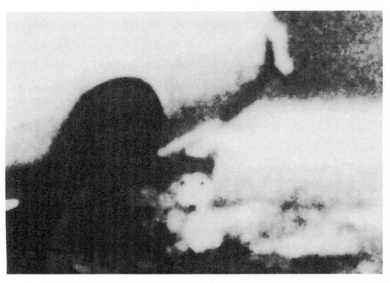

Ghost Husky (photographed by Laurie Shannon Roberts)

Major Wilmot Allistone took a photograph in 1925 which shows a ghostly-looking kitten, as depicted in Fred Gettings' *The Secret of the Cat*. A picture of the Allistone family, taken while they were vacationing in Clarens, Switzerland, shows the head of an almost transparent kitten above the hand of one of the major's sons, casting no shadow, unlike the other objects and people in the photo. According to Allistone, the animal looked like his son's pet, which had been killed by a dog only a few weeks before the photo was taken. Photographic experts at the London Society for Psychical Research could find no indication of fraud.

Robin Armstrong (California) had a gray cat with sapphire blue eyes named Frosty for 15 years. In 1993, the cat started showing signs of diabetes and Robin began giving her insulin shots in the neck each day (later he learned that he could have used dietary methods to try to cure her). In 1994, she died. "I did not see her leave her body, but I did feel her presence after she passed on."

The next day, Robin and his girlfriend, April, took Frosty to a pet cemetery. After some goodbye rituals, they sealed the casket and began burial, taking photos of each other at the gravesite. "I said to April that I wished Frosty would show us her spirit to let us know she's ok," Robin states.

"I had forgotten about my wish when April and I picked up the photos the next day," Robin continues. "We were surprised to see a transparent blue light in one of them and we sought natural explanations. The day was overcast, so glare was ruled out. I had taken three photos within seconds of each other and the camera did not move between shots. Only the last picture had the blue mist. We believe it was Frosty's energy or spirit in answer to our prayer. Later, we were interested to hear that people who claim to see animal spirits sometimes describe them as having a blue color."

Laurie Shannon Roberts (California) has an unusual talent, it appears. "I can't seem to help but take pictures of ghosts when I photograph cemeteries, although I can't actually see anything unusual at the time." A friend who has accompanied her on her photographic expeditions swears that tricks are not involved. Laurie says she just aims the camera and shoots. Some of the ghostly figures appear to be animals.

A photo of Brutus, the elkhound of Ray Tweedy and Leon Thompson of Kent, Washington, is in the Eastman Kodak Album Exhibit at the Statue of Liberty in New York. "He was a well-trained and intelligent dog who liked to walk on his hind legs and would do a lot of comical things," they tell us.

The men had always placed a Christmas wreath in their front window and Brutus would sit looking at the wreath for long periods. The

Christmas after he died they took a picture of the wreath from outside. When it was developed "there was Brutus looking out the window. You can see the rings around his eyes and nose and even the flopped ear on the right side." Unfortunately, the face is tiny, the photo is fuzzy and the picture does not reproduce well.

There is other evidence which suggests that Brutus is still around the house. Visiting dogs seem to react to something invisible at the home and something bumps into their beds each night, just as had occurred every evening when the dog was alive and decided to turn in.

CHAPTER TWO

GHOSTS

Virtually all religions throughout history have believed that the human spirit goes into a dimension at death which we normally do not see, except when environmental circumstances are just right, the witness possesses special perceptive powers or the deceased has an attachment or message which causes him or her to return to the material realm. This is not entirely a matter of faith: numerous individuals in every culture and time have claimed to have encountered these ghosts (42 percent of Americans).

It is only recently, as death impinges less on daily life, that we have tried to ignore it. We pretend that it doesn't bother us and brush it under the rug, asserting that modern people don't need to bother with archaic funeral rituals. As we have bravely tried not to look death in the face, we have cut ourselves off from the supernatural experiences which the rest of humanity has accepted as a fact of life. But the fact remains that people in all walks of life continue to provide testimonials of the intervention of the Other World into ours.

If we count the small traditional native spiritual systems and consider the sweep of history, we can also say that most religions have also accepted as an obvious fact the idea that animals survive death as well. This, too, has been supported by personal experience and the revelations of spiritual leaders. The following reports come from individuals who say they saw the spirit of a pet—sometimes other senses were involved, as well—and acceptance of their testimony rests in either knowing the witnesses or recognizing signs of truth-telling. If they are making up these experiences, why are the incidents described as so fleeting and lacking in grandeur? These individuals did not, of course, know each other at the time of their encounters with the animal dead and few had other supernatural experiences. Those who believe these witnesses are lying or hallucinating probably also reject the stories previously told, where there was contextual evidence to support their testimony. For those afraid of the implications who cling to a materialistic dogma, no amount of evidence is likely to persuade them to open their minds.

Mary Chayer (Alabama), a retired executive secretary for a trade union, believes her boxer Dutchess saved her life on two occasions. The first was in 1945, when Dutchess was a six-month-old puppy. She barked incessantly at a fire in the apartment building where her family lived. "If she had not awakened us, we would not have survived. She was always protective and an excellent watch dog," Mary says of the dog, who died in 1953.

In 1959, Mary was living alone in a basement apartment and decided to do her laundry one Friday night to get a jump on the weekend list of things to do. "As I headed towards my back door to go to the laundry room across the courtyard, I suddenly saw Dutchess standing on the small landing at the top of the steps. I could see right through her cloudy white body. She seemed to be barring my way. This incident gave me the creeps and I changed my mind about doing the laundry that evening."

Saturday morning Mary overslept and was awakened by a woman's scream. "A neighbor and her husband had gone to the laundry room and were confronted by a wino who had crept into the basement laundry room to 'sleep it off'. If I had gone to the laundry room on Friday evening, who knows what might have happened."

Mary adds that she is Presbyterian—a church without a doctrine of animal immortality—and does not drink. She also knows something about image and reality, as an avid photographer. "I know I did not imagine this experience and it is 100% true."

Jeanne LaFever (California) had a black short-haired cat who disappeared one day in 1984. It took a week to find her body, which had been under a bush. A month later, she says she "felt the presence of the cat and while I was standing in my front yard I looked towards the door of the house and saw a dark cloud, about 10 inches around, low to the ground" It hovered there for a couple of minutes and she tried to send it a mental message of love. Then it was gone.

The second similar experience involved an Akita named Hawk, who had to be put down in 1993 after attacking the neighbors and their dogs. She wavered back and forth about the difficult decision after leaving the dog with the veterinarian. When she called back to say she had changed her mind, it had already been put to sleep. Moments later, a cloud appeared over the dining table and she knew it was her dog. "I felt its grief at our separation and I cried for about five minutes in sympathy before the cloud faded away."

Hawk (owner, Jean LaFever)

Jennifer Williams (Pennsylvania) was seven years old when she had a Siamese cat, Coco. She and sister Terri one day found Coco dead by the pond. "I used to sleep in a room by the heating vent. For three months starting shortly after Coco's death, I saw her walk into the room. I was very scared, then I thought it was nice. Finally, I told the cat to go. I didn't tell anyone until I was older because I thought they would believe I was simply imagining it."

Terri Williams (California) also had an experience with a pet who returned from death. She was 18 years-old and living at home in New Jersey when her father shot and killed her terrier beagle, Sniffer, who was 17. He said it was because the dog was old, but she felt he did it because he did not like the dog and she was bitter towards him as a result, and felt guilty about the death of her beloved pet.

Nine years later, Terri was consulting a psychic in Boston when he suddenly paused and said, "This is unusual. There's an animal here and he wants you to know that he is OK and he forgives you." Terri believes Sniffer wanted to let her know that he understood that he was old and that his transition had been at the right time. This prompted her to approach her father and tell him how she felt. He explained that he had not killed the dog out of animosity and he felt terrible that she had so long resented him for the act. "We cried together and it turned out to be a great healing and reconciling experience," Terri says now.

Margarete Beth (California) had a little black poodle named Ebony in 1976. The dog was old and blind in one eye and one night she got out. Eventually, she was found dead on the road. While alive, she would sometimes follow the Beth sisters to school.

"Several times after she died, I also found her walking next to me on the way to school," Margarete recalls. "Then for a couple of weeks she showed up in my classroom, sitting right next to me. She would look up at me and I would tell her to stay there so no one else would see her. I was afraid that if they saw her they would make me take her home."

Then one day, Ebony did not show up and she never saw her again.

If the initial experiences were the result of desperate childhood wish fulfillment, why the sudden departure? Margarete can remember nothing in her life that would account for this. If this were purely imaginative, she would have been more likely to fantasize the dog staying outside the classroom to avoid being taken by authorities.

Faith Cornwall (Tennessee) moved in 1986 to a retirement apartment complex where pets were not allowed. She placed her cat, Cindy, in a new home through the veterinarian. A few months later, Faith was resting on her bed when Cindy suddenly appeared to her. "Her coloring was bright, eyes clear and her expression alive and alert," states Cornwall. "I greeted her and she lay down in the crook of my arm, as she often did when she slept on my bed. Then she disappeared." Faith was unable to determine whether the cat had died, but she certainly saw its spirit, which seemed to return to bid farewell, since Faith has never seen Cindy since.

Gizmo was by all accounts an extraordinary dog. He would be taken to visit hospitals and care homes and knew exactly who wanted attention. His owner, Anita Felix (Arizona), was a veterinary technician. Their bond was profound and she took the dog with her everywhere.

Gizmo (owner, Anita Felix)

Over Memorial Day weekend in 1993, she and a girlfriend were returning from a trail ride and as they approached a blind hill, they were on the right side of the road, but Gizzi was not, so she moved her horse over to block him, as I had done thousands of times before. Unfortunately, the car did not try to veer and he skidded into them. Anita was thrown clear, but Gizzi's throat was torn and he died in her arms. The stress of grief aggravated another medical condition and she had to go into surgery for a hysterectomy a few months later.

"Right before I was anesthetized I felt Gizzi's presence, then saw him," she states. "As I was near death, requiring two units of my own blood donated previously, I believe Gizmo was watching over me. I told him I loved him and to go towards the light, that God wanted him and to look for my father and Beau, another wonderful dog. I know I was neither dreaming nor hallucinating. I could feel him, as well as see him."

Dale Suess, the (human and pet) funeral consultant in Oakland, California, cited previously, had another encounter with a departed dog. Tramp, a Boston-colored Great Dane, had a stroke and the veterinarian said not to move him. Dale, a soup chef at the time, went on to work. At 1:00 p.m. he suddenly felt like someone hit him in the chest and it flashed through his mind that Tramp had died. He rushed home and found the dog dead but still warm.

In the summer of 1984, Dale was suffering from a serious allergic reaction to a food and lay down half conscious. "I remember very vividly seeing Tramp's black and white face come up to the bed. He put his head on my stomach, just like he used to. When I went to pet him, I realized he was dead and I passed out just before I touched his head."

When Dale awoke, he had no more gastro-intestinal problem. "I was not dreaming; I remember quite clearly what happened before I went unconscious," he says.

Katherine Reid (Manitoba), a registered nurse, has bred champion long-haired dachshunds. She was keeping one black and tan puppy and three red dogs in one room, while a black and tan dachshund, Maggie, who was in heat, was locked in a crate in her bedroom. One night as she was retiring, she heard a terrific shrieking and rushed into the other room to get the puppy, who had been nipped by one of the other dogs. She returned to her bedroom to soothe the dog, who was still yelling at the top of his lungs, even though he was really unhurt.

It was then that she noticed Maggie sitting by the side of the bed. Katherine lay down, figuring Maggie would return to her crate on her own. Then it dawned on her that Maggie must have somehow gotten the crate open and needed to be locked up again. When she went over to the crate, there was Maggie locked in her crate and asleep.

"Did the mother of these dogs, Lisa, who looked like Maggie and was dead, return in response to the howling of the puppy?" asks Katherine. "Lisa always was a most unusual dog with a mind of her own."

She adds that she has not told many people this story because when she once asked someone in the Salvation Army if animals had souls, he responded in horror, suggesting that it was sinful to even think they might have.

Like the Terri William story above, in which a psychic said something which could only have been paranormally prompted, Katherine Reid's story has an element, Maggie being inexplicably in and out of the crate, which makes these stories as often as not difficult to dismiss as simple fantasies.

Marla Briggs (California) tells the tale of George, a black labrador who was 17 when the dog had to be put to sleep. "My husband took her to the vet in December 1984 without telling me and I never got the chance to say good-bye," she says. "A week later I was playing with our other two dogs when George appeared and started running and jumping around the yard." The other dogs did not notice George, but she came up to Marla, looked at her for a minute, then disappeared in the blink of an eye. "I felt a great peace and happiness, knowing somehow without a doubt that she was happy and healthy wherever she was." In March

61

1994, George appeared again as Marla was getting ready for work one morning.

Marla adds that she "is not religious and if someone had told me a story like this before my own experience, I would not have believed it. Yet, I now absolutely know we will meet again."

George (owner, Marla Briggs)

"I know that animals survive death because I had five visits from one of my dogs," states Mary Ann Hirzi (California). She had a premonition about getting Queenie, a mix of retriever (in face) and collie (in body, primarily white with beige hair). "I kept seeing a white blur go by while reading the paper. I thought I was imagining things until I picked her out at the humane society and she went right to my car and mixed naturally and immediately with my other dogs."

In February 1990, Queenie passed over. The first visit came a couple of weeks later when Mary Ann saw the dog walk past her into another room. Four other times this happened that year, then nothing until a similar event in 1994. If wishful thinking had anything to do with it, then the visitations should have been more frequent, consistent and recent.

Very down to earth, Mary Ann says she has also seen some human spirits: once each at home, at work, and at a cemetery. "I'm not crazy and I don't drink," she says for the record. If one assumes that she imagined Queenie, it is worth remembering that there was another human witness and several animal ones to the ghostly experiences related by her in the prior chapter.

Dana Komjathy (Connecticut) saw her dog Pebbles several months after the dog died. Pebbles was running across the yard at her mother-in-law's house a number of times. The dog had never been there in mortality, but is buried there.

Then, in September 1990, nine months after Pebbles had to be put to sleep, Dana was watching television when she looked down and next to her on the floor was the dog. Dana closed her eyes and opened them again, just to be sure she wasn't fantasizing, but Pebbles was still there. "I was afraid she would disappear if I touched her, so I just watched her lying there for a half hour before she was suddenly gone."

Three months later, Dana was in a car when she saw Pebbles floating alongside level with the window!

Ellen Cutler (Michigan), had a Chihuahua named Amourcita, which she had euthanized in the dog's 12th year due to cancer. "I remember her accusing expression at the veterinarian," says Ellen 14 years later. "It was an unusual look and I saw it on two other occasions."

One night after Amourcita was put to sleep, Ellen looked up to see her lying across the room in the dog's favorite chair. "She stared at me with that same expression for a minute, then faded away. Another time I was sitting on my couch and suddenly felt something watching me. I looked towards the end of the couch and there was Amourcita looking around the end with that same face. A minute later she disappeared."

If, indeed, Ellen was not simply projecting guilt and imagining an accusing expression, this would imply that, unlike most stories of animals returning after euthanasia, not every pet understands and accepts. That would be consistent with the variations in animal personalities.

Juanita Martinez (New Mexico), the pseudonymous individual cited in the last chapter, recounts a story about a neighbor's dog, Sarah, with whom she developed a close relationship. "I used to baby-sit her when the owner would be away for more than a day. One day when I went over, Sarah was gone and I couldn't find her."

Juanita finally went to the railroad station, knowing the owner had taken the train. "I suddenly noticed Sarah in what looked like a ghostly form bounding down the sidewalk and across the parking lot near the station. She seemed to be happy. I saw her several times in that area."

Soon after returning home, the neighbor called and explained that the dog had followed her to the station and had been killed by a car.

Richard Louden (Indiana), now a factory inspector, had a collie named Pal when he lived on a farm in eastern Indiana as a little boy. "When he died at seven—I was five—I grieved for weeks. Nothing could console me. I couldn't understand where he went or why they wouldn't bring him back. My mom and grandma worried terribly when I wouldn't eat." Note that theological brainwashing cannot be part of the "explanation" for this one.

Then one night he woke up and heard Pal's bark. He thought he was dreaming and tried to go back to sleep, but the barking kept on, Richard says. "I got up on my knees on the bed and looked out the window. The moon was shining bright and there, straight in front of the open window, sat Pal. He was about 15 feet out in the yard in a bubble of sunshine in the middle of the night. A tree limb penetrated the bubble and the leaves inside were as green as day. The leaves outside were silver in the moonlight. Everything behind Pal was in daylight also, the garden, trees and fields beyond. The rest was moonlit." This does not sound like a description which would come from anything but what Richard says is a "very vivid memory."

He says he could actually understand the woofing of his dog. "I knew that he wanted me to know that everything was all right, but that he had to go, that I shouldn't grieve anymore, since he was happy. I know this sounds silly, but I swear I knew this from listening to him." Considering that prior to this experience he could not comprehend what had happened to Pal and had never pretended to understand his dog's barking before, does it seem likely that, weeks into grieving, he suddenly imagined this?

As soon as his master had acknowledged the messages, Pal trotted off down the backyard hill, inside his bubble of light all the way (an unlikely hallucination), until he went over the top of a hill. Richard says he felt "expanded beyond my tender years" and he lay back down to a peaceful sleep.

The next morning, everyone was amazed at the change in him at breakfast. "They said I dreamed it, of course. I know I didn't. I reminded them that they believed that relatives sometimes come to visit the family after they have departed, so why not a pet?"

Brenda Rowan (Washington), a respiratory therapist with an experience in the first chapter, also had a cat whom her husband found dead in the basement one day. "We were shocked and grieved and could not figure out why Lele had died, since she was only six and seemingly in good health," Brenda comments. Over the next year, she saw Lele's spirit three times.

"The first time was when I opened the door and there she was in the hallway and she just scooted away into thin air," Brenda recalls. " The second encounter was similar. Another time I saw her on a fence where she liked to be and she jumped down and disappeared the same way. Each experience only lasted a few seconds, but I knew what I had seen."

What makes these seem unlikely to be the product of wishful thinking is that Brenda never had any visits from the soul of her cocker spaniel, who passed on at 13, a pet she loved much more than Lele.

Olga Newman Adler (Connecticut), who related the story in the first chapter about her living cats reacting to a ghost feline, got a two week old charcoal-with-white-bib kitten when it was abandoned by his mother. He was desperately sick and Olga nursed him to health. "We developed such a rapport that he would do what I wanted before I could put my thoughts into words." She believes this demonstrates the mind of animals, since what Olga wanted the cat to do could not always be deduced from body language, as skeptics would suggest. Her daughter believes she heard the cat speak to her own mind once, though she had doubted her mother's claims of telepathy prior to that.

Fosdick (owner, Olga Adler)

In his 12th year, Foz became ill and had to be put down in 1987. "I saw his little shadow running low on the floor after that," Olga claims. "Then, three years later, I entered my bedroom and there he was, fur coat sleek and shiny, green-yellow eyes glowing, white bib and mittens immaculately clean as in life, though he looked a little bigger and heavier. He was very real and solid-looking. He sat by the window facing me in a shaft of sunlight. I could even see the dust motes dancing in the air above him and he stared at me for 10 seconds. I called his name and he gradually faded from sight." Seeing the detail of dust would not seem to be something likely to hallucinate.

Olga's brother, Tom, rescued a cat from the street he named Tiger. A couple of years later, Tom nursed him lovingly through a near-fatal spinal injury and they became inseparable after the cat's miraculous recovery. A few years later, her brother became ill with cancer. The cat had appeared to be pining for Tom while he was being treated and while seemingly in perfect health, Tiger suddenly died of no apparent cause. Two weeks later, in June 1977, Tom passed away. The family was in tremendous grief for a while.

One day, however, Tom's widow, Mary, who had trance medium abilities, announced that she had awakened from sleep one day and said she saw Tom holding Tiger, "very three-dimensional, like flesh and blood beings. They both looked so handsome, radiant and happy!" The family is convinced that the cat had passed on first in order to greet her Master on the other side.

Another person who swears that "picture conversations" were projected into her mind from animals when she was a child is Keaha Waddell (Texas). Still, it was a surprise when, as an adult, she saw the soul of a pet while it was still living.

One evening in 1990, as she was studying, her three-and-one-half-year-old collie, Sasha, began to make strange sounds in her sleep and Keaha was worried by her labored breathing and irregular heart beat. "As I sat quietly watching her, I was astonished to see a mist rise up out of her body. She didn't move or wake up. I thought this meant she was going to die, but she didn't." The last comment complicates the attempt to dismiss this as an extension of her childhood acceptance that animals had minds. Keaha mistakenly assumed that separation of body and spirit would result in death, so her preconceptions did not mold the experience.

Most interestingly, that very night another of her dogs, Mitzi, died trying to come to the alternative healing clinic where Keaha was recovering from illness. "Perhaps Sasha went to visit her friend in the other world before returning to her body," Keaha speculates. And it should be added, neither dog visited Keaha after they died.

Chantra's Sasha Star (owner, Keaha Waddell)

Judy Spangler (Washington) also believes her dog communicated with her. In October, 1977, her deaf and blind dachshund, Carol, was so debilitated that Judy took her to the veterinarian to be put to sleep. A few days later, the Spanglers moved to a new home.

A couple of months later, Judy looked out her front window and saw Carol waddling up the walkway. Stunned, she opened the door and watched Carol come up to the door. Then Judy swears she heard Carol, in her mind, complain, "You didn't tell me you were moving." Then she felt the dog communicated that she was tired as she lay down. Judy stood there and stared for a few minutes before quietly shutting the door. "I thought I was going crazy," she comments. "When I opened the door later, Carol was gone."

Lynne Morris (Texas), now a composing room foreman at the local newspaper, got her Chinese shar-pei from the local pound. Kaido was in terrible shape, with mange and heartworm, but was nursed to health and became her shadow from then on. One day she watched in horror as a pit bull attacked Kaido, who lingered for two days at the veterinarian's before passing over.

"Maybe it was the tragic nature of his death or the fact that he did not die at home," Lynne theorized, "but in the following year I saw Kaido's ghost three times." Two months after his transition, she was washing clothes in the garage, where he spent much of his time. When she turned around "there was something there, no definite form, like a wavy motion of energy." Her first reaction was terror: she knew it was Kaido, but she ran out of the garage, having never had a supernatural experience before.

The second visit from the dog also took place in the garage, but this time she could not see him clearly, though she distinctly felt his presence.

The third time was in the living room. "Out of the corner of my eye I sensed something in the spot where he used to lie," Lynne states.

She has had no further experiences like this, although she has wanted them. "I never told anyone, for fear I would be laughed at or sent to the nearest nut farm."

Susan Stumpf (Arizona), a psychotherapist, had only one dog, which was a companion for 15 years. Megan was a nervous mixed-breed terrier. In 1990, she had a stroke and after several days it was clear she could not be rehabilitated and was put to sleep out of love. "She made the transition with her head in my hands and my husband and I performed a little ritual to assist in her passing."

They set her ashes on a shelf at home, intending to spread them in the desert nearby that the dog so loved. A year passed and the ashes remained on the shelf. "One week shy of the anniversary of her death, I was home alone one night when I was awakened from a fitful sleep with the sense that someone was in the bedroom," Susan remembers. "I was at first frightened, then as I turned around, there sat Megan in the place right by the bed where she used to sleep. She tapped on the side of the bed with her paw and whined a little and seemed to be trying to tell me something, a motion and sound she often made when she was attempting to communicate her needs." Susan patted the bed, the signal that Megan was to come up on the bed, then reached to pet the dog's neck, but Megan disappeared.

"I lay awake for a while, disturbed that I did not understand what she wanted, but joyful in having seen her again. Although I only saw her for a few seconds, she was quite real and alive as she had ever been. She did not appear ghost-like or shimmering, but solid and vital, although a little worried!" This does not sound like something which could be explained away as the result of being half-asleep. And Susan describes herself as insensitive to psychic phenomena.

Susan and her husband decided to take the ashes and distribute them with a ceremony at the base of a beautiful saguaro cactus in the area the dog liked to play in. Megan never returned from the other realm again.

Geraldine Saram-Jansz (Ontario) and her husband put their dog Maeve to sleep in 1990 because of a tumor. "Several months after Maeve's death," says Geraldine, "we were retiring for the night and I was already in bed reading. Our new puppy, Prince, was getting into his sleeping place at the far end of my long bedside table. I looked down to see how he was doing. To my surprise, there was Maeve, lying curled up close to the bed. She looked comfortable and natural, as if there were nothing unusual in all this."

In a detail which typifies real experience, the kind of thing unlikely to be fantasized, Geraldine recalls that the dog's eyes, black-brown in life, "were white with a piercing, penetrating darker pupil. I was always curious as to why they would look this way."

She believes that the reason Prince did not react to Maeve's ghost was because she was probably already a presence when he arrived two months after her death and he took her in stride by the time Geraldine saw her. Animals do show signs of being more sensitive to psychic phenomena, she points out.

"In 1967, I was inconsolable due to the sudden demise of my constant companion, a dog named Missy," Sandra Gonzalez (Florida) says. "I had Missy since she was five weeks old, when a neighbor's son came to the door with the puppy. I wanted to say no, but as I was talking to him I was holding the puppy, a roly poly mixed Manchester terrier, and the little dog licked my face. I was hooked." After Missy died, she fell into a deep depression over the loss of her friend and was sleeping most of the time.

One afternoon, she awoke and as she sat on the edge of the bed she noticed a dark shadow under a little table by the door. "As my eyes focused, I realized it looked exactly like Missy, and she wagged her tail when I called out her name," states Sandra. "When I stood and walked over to her, however, she just plain disappeared."

"That's all I needed," Sandra now comments. "I knew that Missy had survived, just like humans do. I had been unsure about animals. I know that some day we will be together again. I recovered quickly after that."

Sandra's statement that she was confident about human survival came from another experience. As we have pointed out, some testimonials about pet souls come from people who have no other psychic experiences, while others are like Sandra, who claims to have had a visit by her deceased father when she was nine. One result of this was that her bad leg was cured. "I saw my father as clearly as I see anything in daily life," she asserts.

The late Lee Russ (Arizona) put her Maltese, Tara, to sleep when the dog was 10, due to tumors. "Three-and-one-half hours later I watched her come onto the back porch and sniff around, as she had always done, then go into the front room and lie down in her usual place by my chair."

Two years after that, her other Maltese, Tanya, passed on due to a heart attack. Again, three-and-one-half hours later she showed up, "just sitting there looking at me, then disappeared." Tanya had an independent nature and probably did not want to stick around, Lee wrote about the incident.

Lee then obtained two dogs from a nearby pound. The younger one died within a week. The other, a Pekinese mix she named Mitzi, lived for five years before being put to sleep because of kidney stones. Both dogs appeared to her three-and-one-half hours later.

Skeptics may find the identical timing of the visitations somehow suspicious. However, the fact that there are inexplicable elements in such experiences does not negate their reality.

Antoinette Azolakov (Texas) is described by her sister as "very rational, intelligent, strong and not hysterical." So she was surprised to hear Tony's story one day.

Tony knew her cat, April, a smoke-gray, short-hair with faint darker stripes, had personality-plus right from the beginning, when she put on a tremendous display of cavorting around the cage at the Society for Prevention of Cruelty to Animals where Tony found her. And as soon as April was out of the cage and in the car, she slept for hours. The cat had a remarkable ability to kill scorpions, wasps and bees without getting stung.

In 1972, Tony was living with April in San Antonio where she taught high school English. Then April fell sick from distemper and Tony cradled the cat in her arms all of her last night of life. "She passed on so quietly, I wasn't even really sure when it happened," Tony comments. She laid her cat's body down and went into the kitchen brokenhearted to make some coffee and try to pull herself together.

"As I was sitting at the kitchen table, I saw April trot in from the living room, appearing spry, lively and quite solid. She looked at me and then sprang right through the wall to the outside."

Tony has abandoned teaching to write novels and now has 10 cats. "But I will always remember April, the only one who returned to give me a glimpse of that unseen world beyond the barrier of death."

72

CHAPTER THREE

SENSING THEIR PRESENCE

Everyone knows that the eyes can be tricked, even though many of the visual incidents related in the prior chapter are hard to ascribe to misperceptions. The following anecdotes emphasize experiences involving other senses. Some may regard these as more persuasive than sightings, others may feel they are more subjective and subject to interpretation than visual ones. All add to the mounting evidence that something has really happened to many individuals suggestive of animal immortality.

Rod MacPherson (California) got divorced and right afterwards was sleeping on the floor. His cat, Spunkers (who was the size of a spaniel), would often climb onto his chest. Once he was comfortable, the cat would begin a deep vibratory purring. When Rod moved back to his parents' home, his wife, who worked at a veterinary hospital, took Spunkers and a dog, Missy, and had them put to sleep without his agreement. He was very upset and felt guilty about having let her take the animals.

"About four months later, I had just dozed off one night when I was awakened by a sound like a deep vibration," Rod recounts. "At first I thought it was coming from outside, then it got louder and I could not only hear the rumbling purr of Spunkers, but I felt his considerable weight right next to my left arm." Initially, he was a little unnerved, but once he accepted that the cat had returned to comfort him during a difficult period, he relaxed and went back to sleep.

He woke up several times that night to find Spunkers' presence still with him. At one point around 2:00 a.m., he went to the bathroom and did not hear any sound once he had left the bedroom. "But as soon as I pushed open the door to the bedroom when I returned, I could hear the heavy purring on the bed. I even turned on the light, which did not alter what was happening." He climbed in bed next to where Spunkers seemed to be and went back to sleep.

The next morning the sound and feel of the cat's weight were no longer there and never returned. Given the extended nature of the experience, the two senses involved and the fact that he was obviously not half-asleep when he got up, it would take an unshakable bias to believe that Rod hallucinated the whole thing.

Clairyce Dolson (California) got into breeding golden retrievers with her first one, which had to be put down at age eight because of a progressive mental illness. Then, for several months afterwards, "I would have the feeling of him lying warmly against my feet," she says. "I also experienced the sensation of him standing by my chair, breathing against my arm, and I could smell his breath." The multiple senses involved and repeated experiences strengthen the case for their actuality.

Candice Wolf (California) became involved with mountain lions in 1972. She delivered Tara from her mother, which was owned by a neighbor who bred exotic animals. The mother did not produce milk, so Candice started giving her goat's milk every few hours and slept with her. Tara was raised by a doberman and eventually grew to 140 pounds, compared with a lioness in the wild who usually weighs 90 pounds. She learned to heel on leash and was obedience trained.

When Tara was four years old in 1992, it was raining so hard one day that Candice put a tarpaulin on top of the cage, but the wind blew part of it into the cage and Tara pulled it in and ate some. She died from a bowel blockage.

Tara (owner, Candice Wolf)

Candice was getting up at 3:00 a.m. one morning to feed her dogs, as usual, when she heard Tara's "chirp," just as she sounded every morning during life. From the cage also came the sound of the chain rattling when Tara would jump on a suspended log, although the chain was no longer up. These manifestations continue sporadically. People who have visited Candice's home say they can still feel the lion's presence (even some people who do not believe in the supernatural accept that we can sometimes sense things we can't see, such as "feeling something watching us").

The story of Tara is one of the few anecdotes involving a normally wild animal with a seemingly spiritual essence. Some believe that it is precisely domestication, linking an animal to the soulful human, which allows it to survive death. Since we have few reports about non-pets, it is a question that is still debatable.

Pam Hitch (Missouri) had a shar-pei named Kisha who was "totally in-sync" with her. For example, one day she was shelling eggs in her living room while talking to friends. She went into the kitchen and her friends yelled that the cats were getting into the eggs. Pam told Kisha to watch over the eggs until she returned, which the dog did.

Kisha became ill the week before Christmas of 1994. Pam believes that on the night of December 27, Kisha very clearly spoke to her mind asking to be allowed to go into the next life, so Pam stopped the heroic medical effort to save the dog.

For 10 years, Pam had gone to sleep with Kisha snoring by her bed. Without that sound, Pam found it impossible to sleep for two nights after the dog passed on and she told friends she would give anything to hear Kisha again. On the third night, just as she was falling asleep, she heard the dog's snoring, but it was only after 10 minutes that it dawned on her that this shouldn't be happening, so she got up. The sound stopped, and she did not see a dog. "I went back to bed and the snoring started again," Pam continues. "I decided to start talking to her like I always did. For the next six weeks I went to sleep to the sound of her snoring. Then it just quit. My family thought I was nutty."

Mary Peed (Georgia), who earlier related an incident about her dog, Foxy, reacting to a dog she had previously owned, Tiffany, who had died, also has had other experiences with the latter. She reports that she occasionally feels a same kind of nudge on the blanket over her knees when she is sitting by the window—the same as the dog gave her when she was alive. Mary also feels pressure against her leg when in bed from the corner where Tiffany would always sleep.

Mary points out that she is Episcopalian and therefore has no theological support for her experiences.

Mary Chayer (Alabama), who underscored her own lack of formal religious support for her encounter with a deceased dog in the second chapter, tells of half a dozen non-visual incidents with the soul of her departed cat, Gitano. "He died two days before Thanksgiving, 1978. A year later, I saw something stirring the bedspread right where Gitano would sleep. I also could feel something against my leg. These visits would happen just before someone I knew would die. The last one occurred just before I moved from that apartment in July, 1988."

Dina Andrews, the Purdue University professor of veterinary medicine whose story opened this book, also had some non-visual experiences with deceased animals. One, a female German shepherd named Ellie, used to lie at the top of the stairs in her family's home. After the dog died in 1987, both she and her mother say they definitely sensed the dog's presence in that area (the subtlety of this causes me to categorize it here, rather than as a clear multiple witness experience). "Sometimes we would feel free to walk right through where she used to lie, but other times we just knew there was a physical mass there." And when her parents moved, they encountered the same "presence" in the new home.

There was also some unusual incidents involving a cat she had rescued from the research lab at the University of California at Davis. T'pau was killed in 1990 and Dina did not feel her presence for a month.

Then, as she was stepping out of the truck at the veterinary clinic where she was working late one night, she heard T'pau's distinctive meow. That was the only time she heard this, but on a number of other occasions Dina says she felt something snuggle up to her in bed, just as T'pau had done while alive. Then it stopped as suddenly as it started.

It should be added that Dina never had any afterlife visit from the dog she grew up with and to whom she was most attached, so the above experiences could not be the result of wishful thinking.

Frank Farnswarth (New York), whose first dog, Bobby, was the subject of a story in the multiple witness section, also had his own experience. "After he passed on, I was going to sleep one night when the bed shook, just as it did when he jumped on it, and I distinctly felt him lying next to my legs, as he always did." Was he half dreaming? After Bobby's daughter, Bobbi, died, Frank was wide awake in bed reading a book when the same thing happened. "It was their way of saying goodbye," he concludes.

Kathy West, the Washington veterinary assistant whose family had an extended multiple witness account, had a cat, Buffy, who passed away in 1984. "I was devastated and it felt like I had lost a child," she states. "I had him for 18 years. Then, two days after he died, I was alone in my bedroom with the door shut. I thought I was dreaming that I heard Buffy scratching at the door and I sat up in bed and called out. The door was open just like it always was when he came in and perhaps I heard something in my sleep. Several times after that, I felt something on the bed beside me and I 'knew' it was Buffy."

A couple of years later, Kathy got another cat. The invisible presence of Buffy made itself known one more time and Kathy knew it would be the last. "I could feel his relief that I was taken care of and that he could finally go on. I feel very guilty about this now, because I feel like I kept him from being able to pass over, since he was too worried about me."

Gaynell Wolfe Eller (North Carolina) tells of Lady Blue-eyes, a frost-colored Siamese cat. Lady would awaken Gaynell when she wanted to go outside by jumping up on the bed, walking up her mistress's legs, and rubbing her nose on Eller's chin. If that did not work, she would bite the chin. "That always worked," she comments dryly.

One evening when Lady was let out, she did not come back and for three weeks a search was conducted in vain. Then one night, "I was awakened from sleep by the unmistakable weight of a cat jumping onto my bed. In sharp delight I felt Blue-eyes walk up my legs," Gaynell recounts. "I asked her why she had been gone so long and how she managed to sneak back into the house. I could feel her breath on my chin and the tiny tickle of her whiskers. I heard her silent purr."

But when Clairyce reached out to pet the cat there was nothing there and her weight slowly faded away. "I knew she had come to say goodbye, to tell me not to worry."

Dee Dee Mascetti (California), the psychic whose cats reacted to a ghost cat, also had a non-visual experience in September 1993. One of her cats had been killed by a car and one night she felt something snuggle against her leg in bed in the usual place the living cat would have been. She could feel the purring. But when she put her hand in that spot, nothing could be felt (the objection that being able to feel with one part of the body, but not the other makes no sense, is overruled by the senses).

Shrimpie (owner, DeeDee Mascetti)

Dee Dee's friend, Paul, who once counted himself a disbeliever, related his own encounter of this sort. He was house-sitting for someone whose puppy had fallen down the stairs a short time before and expired. In the middle of the night he was awakened by what he thought was a dog jumping around on his bed. He assumed it was the other dog in the house—except that there was nothing on his bed. And it happened several more times.

"When I was a teenager, we had a German shepherd named Lady," recalls Barbara Perry (Wisconsin). "When she died, I missed her, but was not obsessed. Being younger, I took it in stride."

Then one day when Barbara was very sick, she was lying in the living room half asleep and very uncomfortable. "Suddenly, I felt Lady nuzzle me and lick the side of my face. I felt the distinctive pressure of her tongue on my cheek. When I went to put my arm around her, I was surprised she was not there because the experience was so real." Barbara is convinced Lady returned to make her feel better. "I will never forget this as long as I live."

Clare Hodgins (California) and her husband, who was ill and house-bound, owned a home in San Diego in the late 1960s. Someone left a golden-eyed Burmese kitten, black with copper-tipped fur, in their yard. They named him Leo and he would always sleep on a bath mat on the lower corner of Clare's bed. On cold nights, he would snuggle up against her leg. She and the cat developed a rapport and she was even able to communicate telepathically (she would visualize a place on the porch for Leo to lie down and he would do so, for example). She could tell when the cat was upset and one day she sensed he was in trouble when he did not return from his daily outdoor wanderings.

The Hodgins had to move from their home, but waited a while to see if Leo would return. Eventually, they moved into an apartment. "One night," relates Clare, "I woke up to feel a warm spot against my leg on the outside of the covers where Leo used to lie on cold nights. It felt like him and when I looked, there was a golden glow in that area, a little larger than he had been. I thanked him and blessed him, knowing he was no longer among the living." Although she saw something, touch seems the predominant sense.

Dana Komjathy (Connecticut) is clairaudient, she claims, hearing supernormally at times. On two occasions she says she heard the very distinctive bark of Pebbles, her departed cocker-poodle. These impressions were reinforced by other senses: "After the barks woke me up one morning, I felt her climb into bed with me and I was able to hold her and smell her, although I saw nothing. It was a wonderful visit." One bark could be imagined, but the other senses, repetition and extended nature of the experiences make it hard to fathom how all of this could be fantasy.

Olga Newman Adler (Connecticut), who saw living and ghost cats play together as reported in chapter one, also says she would "hear the bed depress slightly where my cat Bogar used to sleep, then hear his slight creak and see the top cover move, as if a small body were settling down."

Then there was Olga's cat Red Phantom, who was so heavy the floor would creak as he walked across it and he was very noisy climbing into the litterbox, scratching around and getting out. Since he died in 1992, Olga has often heard some phantom walking the floor, using the litterbox and voicing Red's throaty plaintive purr.

Nelly Gonzalez (Florida) had wonderful communication with the kitten she received when it was six weeks old. Evidence of how far this could be taken occurred when Nelly was at work one day. She suddenly saw Peke's face appear in front of her for a few moments like a vision. When Nelly got home, she found the house burglarized. The cat had seemingly been frightened into an extraordinary effort to contact her mistress.

"Exactly one week after Peke's death at nearly 15," Nelly recounts, "around 9:00 p.m. at night, I was on the phone with a friend, who was giving me support in my grieving. While we were talking, I became aware of some noises in my dining room. There and in the kitchen are the only areas where I have tiles. I could hear an animal scratching, just as Peke would do when she didn't like being confined to the tile area."

K. C. Cowen (Idaho) was living in California when she found a black kitten which seemed close to death one hot day. Among his many other problems, he turned out to have only one lung, causing a rattling sound when he breathed. She nursed "E.A. Poe" back to health, having become an expert on animal nutrition and with a psychic talent for healing animals, although the odd breathing remained.

When the Cowens moved to Flagstaff, Arizona, the cat and dogs loved to run in the outdoors, but she always supervised Poe so that he would not get harmed. Then one night he sneaked by as she was letting the dogs out and did not come back.

The next morning she found the body, leading to the first unusual experience. "The body was covered with blood, so I went back to the house to get a towel. When I returned, I was stunned: there was not a drop of blood anywhere and the body was totally intact."

Four days after Poe's death, K.C. was sitting in the living room and felt a chill. She got up to put wood into the stove, remembering how Poe liked to lie with her three-and-one-half-year-old female pointer, Poppy, right by the stove. "Suddenly, I heard Poe's rattle and looked over at Poppy, who was curled on his bed in the way he would lie when Poe was next to him." Then the rattle stopped, but she heard it again when she was feeding the dogs (Poe used to sit on the counter top and wait for his food there) and twice more by the stove. "Each time I told him I was happy he had come back to ease my grief and I said how much I missed him."

The late Lee Russ (Arizona), whose story was told in chapter two, had a Doberman pinscher, Teret, who had to be put to sleep at 13 after suffering an illness. "The next morning, I heard her jump from the bed as usual, toenails clicking as she walked on the tile floors," Lee wrote.

One could be inclined to believe that Lee imagined this, but she said that this continued for several months.

Judie Hurta (Wisconsin), whose sighting of a friend's deceased cat was detailed in chapter one, had three cats in 1974, the youngest one named Smokey, who was in constant mischief. He had an unusual meow, "kind of a whisper," Judie recalls. "I've never heard one like it since, and I've had lots of cats." Just before they were moving, Judie let the cats out, but Smokey did not return. The family looked for him frantically the next day to no avail.

That night while everyone was watching TV, Judie heard Smokey's meow. "I went to the back door and he wasn't there, but I kept hearing him. The lower I put my head to the floor in the kitchen the louder he sounded. I called him at the heating vent and I could hear him as if he were next to me." She was convinced Smokey had gotten into the vent, although only her son claimed to hear anything unusual at all (the preponderance of evidence here is one person hearing, not multiple witness). Her husband refused to help, saying the cat was gone and she was imagining things, but Judie continued to hear the cries for days.

"I hated to leave him, but it was time to move and there seemed nothing we could do," explains Judie. "One day a year later, my husband brought some buddies home, one of whom had Smokey's brother. I overheard my husband tell him that a neighbor had seen Smokey run over and brought him the body. He knew how I would react and decided not to tell me, burying our cat alongside the garage."

CHAPTER FOUR

GLIMPSES FROM THE OTHER SIDE

We think of our civilization as the culmination of history and believe that we have achieved much greater enlightenment about the nature of reality than our ancestors. Yet on many issues, what is accepted as the truth by the intellectual establishment or society at large is demonstrably contrary to the facts which our predecessors recognized. The examples range from medicine to archaeology and dissidents feel like the boy in the *Emperor's New Clothes*, knowing that consensus reality is foolish.

One of those areas of cultural stupidity involves death. Our fear of annihilation would be considered a silly thing, contrary to all experience, by most of the billions of people who have ever lived. Only in the past couple of decades have we begun to pay more than once-a-week lip service to the notion of a parallel dimension, a place where spirits exist which can be seen or visited under special circumstances while still alive. It makes sense that if we are to seek evidence of such a place, we will have to depart from our traditional close-minded intellectual armchairs. The perspective the following approaches provide us is actually from that other side of reality or looking into it, as opposed to witnessing something which has invaded this dimension. Hardcore skeptics of the supernatural will want to exit immediately.

In 1975, Raymond Moody's *Life After Life* was published, the first popular and comprehensive examination of so-called near-death experiences (NDEs), situations when individuals clinically die, then return to life, often with remarkably similar stories about their souls leaving their bodies and momentarily entering the realm of the dead. Moody went on to write two other best-selling books on the subject, *Reflections on Life After Life* and *The Light Beyond*. Others have followed in his steps and the evidence for the objective reality of these experiences compiled in volumes such as Melvin Morse, M.D.'s *Close to the Light* and *Transformed by the Light*, Colin Wilson's *Afterlife*, Kenneth Ring's *Life at Death*, Elizabeth Kubler-Ross's *On Children and Death* and Michael Sabom, M.D.'s *Recollections of Death* is impressive. The central themes of leaving the body and going on a brief journey into another realm where the dead are still alive is fairly uniform, with details apparently affected by cultural conditioning. Most interesting are the experiences of children who have had little or no religious instruction.

Those who try to shrug off the evidence are of two kinds. Most simply have not read the material, making uninformed judgments about its importance or validity, their comfortable intellectual world blissfully undisturbed by new information. Others approach the evidence with such prejudice, obviously feeling threatened by such reports, that nothing could convince them (not necessarily even the experience of dying, if frequent reports of spirits refusing to accept the reality of their death are true).

Skeptics have tried to explain away NDEs without listening to the answers provided by researchers. For example, some have suggested that the near-dead only fantasize that they are out of their bodies observing what surgeons are doing to revive them, in reality incorporating doctors' conversational tips into their hallucinations. But when such cueing is controlled, those who are resuscitated still come back with the same reports. More important, people who have come back from death often are able to detail conversations held elsewhere or report observations of things outside the surgery room. No alteration of brain chemistry could account for this.

Many of the NDEs occur when no brain wave EEG registers and therefore there could be no hallucinations, since they would produce brainwaves (the movie "Flatliners" is a fictional story of young doctors who subject themselves to experiments in which they leave their bodies while their EEG is flat). In fact, in NDE experiences where a brain wave does register, it has been noted to have changed at the precise moment when the resuscitated individual claims to have left the body. Brain wave changes also occur during out-of-body experiences, also known as astral projections or exteriorizations, while those who experience it are still alive and NDE-type events can also be induced through stress short of death.

In 1992, while I was researching this book, I asked parapsychologist D. Scott Rogo, who had recently written an acclaimed study of NDEs, *The Return from Silence*, why it was that books about the subject did not mention animals in this other world. He had discovered two accounts which were exceptions. In one, a young boy who had temporarily died stated that when he crossed over he had been greeted by his deceased dog and cat. In the other, a 38 year-old woman described finding herself in this other dimension where she saw a butterfly; then a deer came up and licked her face and she was pulled back into her body.

It turned out that the lack of reports about animals in the hereafter was due to the fact that researchers had not bothered to ask anyone about this issue. Melvin Morse did mention in passing in *Transformed by the Light*, that a child had tried to climb a heavenly fence to get at some horses, but the general silence was not shattered until Betty Eadie's *Embraced by the Light* became a bestseller in 1993. In it, she records having moved through the famous "tunnel" towards the light with other people as well as animals. Later, she says she was shown animal spirits being created before being put into mortal bodies.

It is particularly interesting that although Eadie was baptized a Mormon a decade before her experience, she had not been active in the church and was completely unaware that it had a doctrine that animals had spirits which were created before the animals were born. In a collection of near-death experiences reported by Mormons, *Glimpses of Eternity* by Alvin Gibson, references to otherworldly animals include birds and butterflies. In *Beyond Death's Door*, an analysis of the meaning of NDEs from the Mormon standpoint, Wendy and Brent Top comment that the few recorded examples of encountering such animals usually involve children, and they cite a non-Mormon example in which a 10 year-old girl saw the "shadow" of a departed pet dog and was led back to her body by a lamb.

Robert Liardon's *I Saw Heaven* is a disarmingly candid story of the author's NDE at age eight from the perspective of a born-again Christian, first published in 1983. Disregarding the views of many fundamentalists, he reports having seen a dog, goat, lion and numerous birds *Over There*.

Betty Preston of Seattle (like Betty Eadie, Melvin Morse and some other key figures in this field) underwent heart surgery in 1975 and reported a similar experience during a coma. "Suddenly, I was floating through a tunnel with other people and animals," she began relating the traditional experience. "I knew that we were all dying. At the end of the tunnel was a light that was coming towards me."

F. Brown, a retired California teacher, became very ill when she was nine. She remembers "dreaming" that she and her kitten went to meet her mother, who had died when Brown was three. The girl was told that she had to "return" because she still had work to do. Her cat stayed with her mother.

Brown woke up screaming at 3:30 p.m. that day. Her father was astonished, since she had been declared dead at 10:30 a.m., after three days of unconsciousness, by two medical doctors. A blizzard had prevented the coroner from getting to the home. Later, her father told her that while she was sick the kitten she had seen remain with her mother had died.

Recently, Dr. Milton Hadley, a psychiatrist formerly associated with England's Cambridge University, revealed that he had compiled hundreds of accounts of pet encounters during NDEs based on extensive interviews, although few have been released.

One Hadley subject, George T., was declared dead for 19 minutes during open-heart surgery. He says that he remembers "walking through thick white fog towards a light in the distance. As I got closer the fog began to clear. Up ahead, I could make out a large shaggy dog rushing at me, barking. He leapt on me, licking my face, panting and wagging his tail with delight. I realized it was Skippy, a sheepdog I'd had when I was a kid. Behind him I saw a Pekinese named Buffy we had some years back, and Blackie, an old alleycat I had to have put to sleep only four months earlier."

Another Hadley interviewee was a 26 year-old tropical fish collector who "died" after a motorcycle accident. After revival, he testified that he had swum in an otherworldly lagoon surrounded by his deceased fish.

Dr. Melvin Morse, in his volume about children's NDEs, hypothesizes a biological mechanism facilitating the process of leaving the body. Drawing on his own and Chilean research, he argues that the Sylvian fissure in the right temporal lobe of the brain is the "seat of the soul," the place where the electrical activity can be detected when individuals report going out of the body.

What he does not mention is that primates, dolphins and other higher animals have a brain fissure which functions similarly to the Sylvian in humans. But even if they lack this, that would not preclude animals having other mechanisms for separating spirit from body, which would have to be the case if one accepts eyewitness reports of lower animals in spirit form.

Another source of information could be from beings who allegedly inhabit this other world. Understandably, some people will be put off by the notion of relying on those who claim to be psychic channels or mediums because there has been so much fraud in the field and, much more pervasive, so many self-declared psychics who obviously have little paranormal ability. Still, some of these communications are hard to explain in a mundane way and it makes perfect sense that if someone survives death he or she might try to contact the living.

A warning, however: *don't try this at home. That is, conducting seances, using Ouija boards and other attempts to initiate contact with the dead can be dangerous and unreliable.* This is potentially hazardous physically, psychologically and spiritually. Even if spirits are seemingly benign, being dead does not make someone any smarter. These beings could mislead out of ignorance, some seem to be as egotistical as mortals and want to be perceived as sources of divine wisdom, while others may have a hidden agenda. Still, it is important to objectively examine all the evidence for animal survival. Communications purporting to be from the next life have to be assessed as objectively as possible.

Psychic medium George Anderson is by all accounts no charlatan. The subject of bestsellers by Joel Martin and Patricia Romanowski, *We Don't Die*, *We Are Not Forgotten* and *Our Children Forever*, he also does not initiate contact with the dead. They seem to come to him unbidden and have done so since a nearly-fatal childhood illness changed his visual ability so that he apparently sees the other dimension almost constantly. He is usually given no tips in advance about the people who consult him, but is still able to pass on information to the living which is only later verified as accurate, something well beyond any parlor trick. Quite frequently, he has also reported seeing animals in the immortal world.

In the first book, he is described doing a reading for a friend of the authors, Joan. Her mother, Anderson said, appeared to him and he determined she had recently died. He asked Joan if the mother had a dog which had also passed on, because the mother told George that the dog had been there to greet her when she died and it helped make the transition easier. Joan confirmed that was the case.

Why would a pet meet the newly deceased? One reason Anderson suggested in the second volume is that the person would follow the animal to wherever he or she is supposed to go, trusting that it would only guide the master to a safe place.

Anderson was the subject of a frequently repeated episode of television's popular "Unsolved Mysteries" in 1992, on which was recreated a reading for the Licata family, whose son David had been killed in a hit-and-run accident (the original reading is related in detail in *We Don't Die*). Anderson stated that he saw David surrounded by animals and reported that David was telling him that he worked with animals on the other side. The family verified that in mortality David was fond of animals.

What they did not tell Anderson was that the family dog, which they did not name, had died. Four years later, in a follow-up reading, Anderson was bewildered by what he claimed David was telling him an important symbol for Mrs. Licata: a muffin (for some reason, Anderson often receives his information via symbols). Without saying anything to George, she had wanted to know if the dog, named Muffin, was with David.

In *Unknown But Known*, the late medium Arthur Ford mentions a peculiar detail about the nationally-televised seance which he conducted for maverick Episcopal Bishop James Pike, who wanted to get in touch with his son, James, Jr., who had committed suicide. One of those allegedly with the son was an old man who, Ford said, wanted James, Jr., to check out something which would prove his identity. He had two cats with him in that spiritual dimension which were once pets of his son. The son, a Cambridge University professor, verified their descriptions

90

and date of death, which suggested that, indeed, the cats had survived the transition.

David Guardino, a flashy Las Vegas-based "psychic to the stars," turns serious on the subject of seances he has conducted. He claims that deceased human beings "have all told me they met their pets" when they died. He adds that "no pet is capable of breaking one of God's universal laws, which is why all of them—dogs, cats, horses, canaries or goldfish—go to Heaven."

Beatrice Lydecker, probably the world's best-known psychic who claims to read animal minds, undeniably has some kind of talent, as those who have watched her provide accurate descriptions of pets' lifestyles will testify. Some of her experiences are described in her two books, *What the Animals Tell Me* and *Stories the Animals Tell Me*. She also acts as a medium, passing on messages she says she receives from deceased pets to their former owners.

Parapsychologist Ian Currie, author of *You Cannot Die*, concurs, based on seances he has conducted. During one session, a deceased Frenchman allegedly told the medium that as soon as he passed over he felt something nestling against him. When he opened his eyes, he discovered it was his horse, which had died earlier.

In another session, Currie says the clairvoyant contacted the dead woman, who said that within minutes of her death, she was "happily romping with her dog, which had been killed by a car several years earlier, which was now in perfect shape."

Brad Steiger, author of many books on the paranormal, including *Man and Dog*, *Strange Powers of Pets* and *More Strange Powers of Pets*, has also attended many seances in which the dead were said to have met their pets again. "One woman said that when she opened her eyes after dying, on her lap she found her pet cat, gently purring, which had died some years before." His books contain other anecdotes confirming survival.

The late British spiritualist *extraordinaire*, Harold Sharp, author of

Animals in the Spirit World, even seemed to be able to bring deceased pets from that dimension physically into this one. His first such experience was during a seance attended by eight people. Suddenly, a blue-green mist appeared over the heads of the group and condensed into the spirit of a budgie, which settled on the shoulder of one participant, Robert Owensby. Owensby confirmed that it was his former parakeet, which chirped, "I want a cigarette," the constant refrain of Owensby himself, a habitual smoker.

In another session, Sharp concentrated on a big dog, named Hector, he had as a child. To Sharp's surprise and that of his guests, Hector actually materialized. There was a large china bowl of water on the floor and the dog lumbered over to it and began drinking, as if to remind Sharp of the dog's old habit of drinking large quantities of water. Were the attendees of this session simply imagining things? Before leaving, the dog barked loudly enough that two women next door complained.

A somewhat novel approach to contacting the dead was designed by Dr. Raymond Moody of NDE fame. On "The Oprah Winfrey Show" of October 18, 1993, a writer-producer for Turner Broadcasting System told about his use of the Moody method (basically, relaxing in a dark room with a mirror). An initial skeptic, he was not positive that the human spirit he sensed was actually his father, but he was definite about having seen his departed dog.

OUT OF THE BODY

Another way of seeing things on the other side of the Great Divide would be out-of-body experiences (OBEs), also known in spiritualist parlance as astral projections. Scott Rogo, in *Psychic Breakthroughs Today*, documents some of the many scientific experiments which have shown that this phenomenon cannot be explained away as chance or trickery, and he demolishes the criticisms of skeptics. Nor was Rogo's viewpoint based on mere theory: his *Leaving the Body* provided a menu of techniques he had used himself. When he would go to New York, for example, he would often go back to his Los Angeles home in spirit to check on things. Later, when he flew back in body, he would validate his observations made when he was out of the body. Again, one needs to be prudent: there are cases where intentionally-induced OBEs have resulted in nearly-successful attempts by unknown forces to prevent people from returning to their bodies.

One reluctant astral traveler was Irene Swenda (Florida). In the 1960s, while working for the Joint Chiefs of Staff, Operations ('not a place to work if you are psychic because people have a real fear of such abilities"), Irene engaged in Zen meditation and suddenly developed what she described as "alarming psychic powers." Among these were periodic spontaneous out-of-body experiences. "After some startling OBEs and at the request of some close friends, I was able to induce some control," she relates. "I lost a lot of sleep, scared myself half to death, engaged in protracted battles with 'entities' who were intent on possession, and unwittingly drove a near-neighbor out of her apartment, which I had to pass through to reach my target."

In 1976, as Irene was dropping off to what she thought was sleep, she suddenly realized that a very large dog was pressing against her back. With past astral experience suggesting that it was unwise to make quick moves, she reacted cautiously. She could feel the dog panting against her and half rose, reached behind and put her hand on its side. The white long-hair was drenching wet and seemingly badly frightened. It came to her mind that the dog had drowned in Great Falls, Maryland. "Like some humans who are confused when they first pass over, he was unaware that he was 'dead' and finding me offered him some measure of comfort," Irene theorizes.

Adrienne Paradis (California) acquired a tiny black kitten with big yellow eyes when someone separated him from his mother too early, dropping him in a friend's car. Adrienne fed the kitten with an eyedropper and he grew up so limber and lively she called him Ninja. He became inseparable from another of her felines, Remus. One summer's night, she locked what she thought were all her cats inside the house and went to bed. The next morning, she realized that Ninja was missing. She spent three weeks searching for him in vain.

"Then early one morning I heard Ninja's unmistakable meow," Andrienne states. "I woke up and saw him on top of the dresser where he liked to be. I called out to him to come jump onto the bed, which he did. My joy was overwhelming as I sat up, picked him up and held him and kissed him, smelling his fur. I told him I knew he would come back." Then she realized something was wrong. Ninja communicated that he loved the family, but that it was time for him to go and he faded in her arms.

It was only when Adrienne started to lie back in her bed that she realized she was sitting up out of her body. "I have also had experiences with dreams and astral projection throughout my life and I know the difference. That's why I was able to interact with Ninja's second body, which was as real and tactile as if he were alive."

"I learned more about the Universe in those few moments than all the books, lectures and teachers in my lifetime," continues Adrienne. "I now know that there is life after death for animals as well as humans. Our love for each other transcends that mystical gateway."

Dana Komjathy (Connecticut), cited previously, claims to have met her dog, Pebbles, several times while out of the body. The first came in September 1990, about nine months after she had to put the poodle-cocker mix to sleep to end her suffering from congestive heart failure.

"I found myself in this other dimension with Pebbles. There was a waterfall and a river there and we went swimming together," Dana remarks. The incredulous should know that American Indians and other animists consistently describe at least one dimension like an idealized version of this world, whether a creation of the mind or a place that is physical in some sense. "I introduced her to the spirit guide who has often accompanied me in out of body experiences and he remarked how radiant she was. We walked up a path and then Pebbles ran ahead into a mist. I started to go after her, but my guide told me I was to stay behind."

Another woman who has had paranormal experiences all her life, Jane Blair (Tennessee), who is of Native American ancestry, says she has been into another dimension many times. Twice she found herself accompanied by two long-departed dogs: Queenie, a collie she had when living on a farm in Illinois, and Freckles, a cocker spaniel she owned while living in Alexandria, Virginia, where the "exteriorizations" took place.

Jane also had a pure white Arabian horse, Chieftain, and years after his passing, she found herself "riding him in the astral world, traveling like the wind." It happened many times, she says, and "I can still feel the strength of his movement and the ripple of his muscles, and I can see his snowy mane blowing in the wind."

Was this a figment of her imagination? The last time, 15 years ago, she had been questioning how "real" these rides were. Then she found herself "riding across sand dunes in some astral Middle East and upon wakening, I found pure white sand beneath my fingernails. I knew then that Chieftain was truly alive and well."

Gregory Kasperek (Arizona), an assistant manager of security at a resort, visited his brother in Utah in May of 1989. With considerable astral experience under his belt, he decided to go out of his body early one morning when there was a full moon. As he rose above the house, he was surprised to see his brother's dog, Sophie, who he knew was sound asleep in his brother's bedroom, chasing after him in her second body and barking furiously. "She was frustrated because I was able to rise above her reach." Perhaps the dog did not realize the power of its own spirit to rise up, probably not comprehending that it was even out of the body. Gregory recalls the whole experience as one of his best, "in full color, and I was completely lucid the entire time, making choices and trying out new things."

The last category of experiences would be visions of the spirit world, seen from our mortal one. As with other paranormal incidents, many of these are very brief, though loaded with significant implications. By and large, these are the most difficult to validate, but they add yet another straw to the back of the pseudo-rationality which denies such things happen.

Carolyn Brand (Arizona) first heard tales of ghost animals when she worked at a Pasadena, California veterinary hospital in the 1950s, but her own experience did not come until four decades later.

In June 1990, Carolyn had a German/Australian shepherd, Shadow, who was in such pain that the veterinarian advised that the dog be put to sleep. Ten days after this was done, Carolyn was meditating and suddenly she had "a color vision of Shadow running in some tall moist grass; I could only see part of his body and he seemed to be running away from me."

A few days later, as Carolyn was reading the Sunday paper, "I had a second and last vision, also in color; Shadow seemed to be looking down at our world and did not seem to see me." She did not mind this, glad that he seemed to be living another life free from pain.

Betty Smith (Manitoba), a witness in a prior chapter, has another tale to tell. "After Holly, our eldest elkhound, had to be put down at age five, I was home feeling terribly said when I heard a voice say, 'The spirit has been released, she is now free!' and an uplifting feeling came over me. That night, as I sent prayers for Holly into the next world, I was shown a pathway and in the distance a man and dog came toward me. It was twilight and a soft misty glow was around them. As they came closer, I could see a leash of lights from his hand to Holly, a beautiful sight, and I knew someone was taking care of her."

Lucy Nelson (California) feeds 100 cats and says she has had many

Win-Melca's Howdi Holly (owner, Betty Smith)

paranormal experiences. One occurred when a kitten passed away in her arms and Lucy received a vision of "a lovely garden where at first the kitten was bewildered by her new surroundings, but gradually other kitties came to welcome her and she was quite happy."

Roseanne Graff (Michigan), who told us already about the visit of her ghostly dog Sam, found herself grieving for the abuse of all animals one day when a vision of the afterlife was given to her. She says she saw "a beautiful land of awesome green pastures, luscious foliage, great trees, incredibly clear water and huge waterfalls." Herds of wild animals, some extinct, roamed the valleys and hills, "birds of all kinds sang joyously and there were no stinging insects or infirmities." She was told that Noah was in charge, assisted by Job (a surprise to her, until she looked up the biblical story of his care for animals in this world). This vision does have interesting implications regarding wild animal souls and those of insects.

Awakening on another morning, Roseanne was also shown a vision of the departed spirits of Beau, her Tennessee Walkinghorse, and Alfie, her Wolfhound, visiting her living horse, Ruby, in the stable.

The Graffs also had Link to Glory, a three-year-old thoroughbred filly of fastidiousness nature (if her water were even slightly tainted she would bang the tub until it was changed). She also showed unusual courage and curiosity, even as a foal, challenging adult horses and boldly investigating strange things which sent the other horses running. Southern Sun was a retired Tennessee Walkinghorse show animal who helped raise Link and who, Roseanne believes, died of a broken heart after seeing Link buried. Roseanne's mother partially shared a vision of these two immortal horses (although a multiple witness case, this shares more in common with other visions).

Baby, a/k/a, Link to Glory (owner, Roseanne "Pat" Graff)

Shortly after their passing, the Graffs were sitting in the living room and drifted into a relaxed and meditative state in which they saw Sun and Link together in a beautiful pasture. "Sun came closer and conveyed the message that he had completed what he needed to learn from earth," Roseanne recounts. "Link remained more distant, but said he would return to 'fulfill the promise,' although I have no idea what this meant." Although one could debate the sense of an animal coming into this life for the purpose of significant learning, the last point is intriguing both in substance and because it seems an odd thing for her mind to make up when she has no grasp of the meaning.

Beatrice Lydecker, the pet psychic, relates the story of her first German shepherd, Princess Royal, who died in 1968, in *What the Animals Tell Me*. While she was lying on her bed, she says a vision opened up to her and she saw Princess romping through a beautiful forest and swimming in a stream before conveying to Lydecker that she was happy.

Gladys Ewing (Oregon) remembers her dog Sniffie as very smart. One Easter, Gladys had hidden some chocolate eggs for the family, which Sniffie found. But rather than eat the tempting treats, the dog put one on each person's bed in the house!

In 1962, Gladys's husband was transferred by the Navy from their California home to Japan. They had to travel by ship and the dog was kept separate in an area that was cold and windy. He took sick as a result and a few months later died. While lying on her bed one afternoon shortly thereafter, sobbing as she missed Sniffie, Gladys looked up and "saw a large gray curtain in the sky opened by very tall women, dressed in gray, three on each side. When the curtain parted, I saw my dog rolling and playing with another dog in the most beautiful grass I have every seen." She was particularly struck by how shiny Sniffie's coat looked, better than it had every looked in life. Then the curtain slowly closed and Gladys says she heard "the most beautiful music imaginable" before the vision disappeared.

A few days later, her sons came home from school and told her that a friend was leaving for the States and could not take his dog on the plane. They asked if they could take it—and it turned out to be the very dog which Gladys had seen playing with Sniffie in the heavenly world.

Did she actually see Sniffie with the new dog, Erick, in astral form, as a way of both telling her Sniffie was all right and a sign to take Erick? Was it a preview of a time a couple of years later after Erick passed on? In another vision she says she saw yet a third dog, which has never come into the household (the result of a twist of free will?). Whatever the interpretation, Gladys is certain of one thing: "I know there is life beyond for both humans and animals because I saw it."

Death-bed visions, which Rogo and others have shown cannot generally be explained away as hallucinations induced by drugs or the biochemistry of death, also make a contribution to our knowledge of animal survival.

Roxanne Morgan (California) tells the story of her father's death at home. "He was free of pain and medications and described to me the light, the beauty, long-time friends and his mother and my mother appearing to him," she recounts. "Then he said a big black dog crossed the astral barrier and came into the room with us. At first he was annoyed that I could not see it, then said it was sad I could not see the flowers either." She believes the dog was a guide as her father prepared to travel between the worlds.

Nancy Boswell (Idaho) relates what her mother told her about the death of Nancy's older sister. Her mother was at the foot of the bed where her daughter lay when the child suddenly looked up and said, "Look! My kitten came back!" The kitten had died two weeks previously. She also asked who the man was who was standing by the side of the bed. The mother said she saw neither the kitten nor the man and asked her dying daughter to describe the man. The description was of the child's grandfather. She had never seen a picture of him (he died when her father, his son, was two years old).

CHAPTER FIVE

WHAT RELIGIONS SAY

In our not too distant past, there were religious debates about whether members of certain racial or ethnic groups, or even women, had eternal souls. But animals have never even advanced far enough to be seriously considered. It is an astonishing example of the arrogance of the human race that many religions have given little thought to the ultimate destiny of most inhabitants of the planet.

This is not to say that many religions do not teach reverence for life. Some of the strongest statements about the importance of kindness to beasts can be found in the teachings of Islam and the Baha'i Faith, as cited in *Replenish the Earth* by Lew Regenstein, although orthodox adherents reject the notion of brute souls. When it comes down to whether animals are immortal, many major religions have simply assumed a negative position or ignored the question altogether. The evidence now emerging about animal survival is a challenge to bring their theologies in line with human experience. In some cases, however, official dogmas do not square their own scriptures.

BIBLICAL BASIS

As the New Testament reports, the principal antagonistic sects among the Jews at the time of Jesus Christ were the Pharisees, who believed in human immortality, and the Sadducees, who did not (they believed that the scriptures said nothing definitive about any afterlife).

Judaism in its various forms today still has a divergence of opinion, with the most orthodox tending to believe in resurrection or reincarnation and the most liberal merely hopeful for some kind of human survival. Under the circumstances, one could hardly expect a general Jewish religious acceptance of animal immortality, although Judaism has a strong tradition of humaneness.

Still, there are some verses on which one could build a belief in animal spirits in the Old Testament, known to Jews as the Torah, the Prophets and the Writings. Using an English translation of the Bible does not necessarily tell one what the original-language manuscripts that exist today really say, much less what was contained in the original manuscripts (known as autographs). Added to that is the fact that translators use different sets of manuscript copies (Septuagint, Targum, Vulgate, etc.). Because most words can have several meanings, what is relevant is to look at how the same Hebrew words are used to discuss people and animals when it comes to the issue of what gives them life. Remember that translators often cannot or do not translate literally, which can allow their particular biases into their work which may cloud the original teachings.

Most renditions of Genesis 1:30 simply state that God gave "life" to animals. But in Hebrew the words used are "nephesh chay," which in 2:7 is said to mean "living soul" when it comes to the creation of humankind. The same phrase is used again concerning animals in Job 12:10. Genesis passages where "nephesh" is usually translated as "creature" when it comes to animals are 1:21 and 24, 2:19, 9:10,12,15 and 16, while the term is arbitrarily rendered "soul" when applied to people. In Numbers 31:28, however, the King James Version of the Bible does render "nephesh" as "soul," applying the term to both people and animals in discussing payment of a divine tribute.

Numbers 16:22 and 27:16 introduce Hebrew "ruwach," translated as "spirits," in referring to "the God of the spirits of all flesh." Ecclesiastes 3:21 uses "ruwach" to suggest that whatever happens to beasts at the time of death is also the fate of humankind (see verse 19). Although the King James Version uses "breath" in v. 19 and "spirit" in v. 21, the Hebrew uses "ruwach" in both instances.

Ecclesiastes 3:21 also uses "ruwach" for both man and animal as it asks: "who knows whether the spirit of the sons of men goes upward and whether the spirit of the animal goes downward to the earth?" (Septuagint, Vulgate, Syriac and Targum manuscripts; garbled and incorrectly translated in the King James Version).

Hebrew "neshamah," which can be defined as "spirit" and is rendered in English as "breath of life," is used in Genesis 7:22, referring to both the people and animals who died in the Flood.

There are also a few relevant scriptures in the New Testament.

Romans 8:19-23 states "19. for the earnest expectation of the creation eagerly waits for the revealing of the sons of God. 20. For the creation was subjected to futility, not willingly, but because of Him who subjected it in hope; 21. because the creation itself *also* (italics added) will be delivered from the bondage of corruption (decay, death) into the glorious liberty of the children of God. 22. For we know that the whole creation groans and labors with birth pangs until now. 23. Not only *that*, but we also who have the first fruits of the Spirit, even we ourselves groan within ourselves, eagerly waiting for the adoption, the redemption of our body." (New King James Version, and see *The New Testament from 26 Translations* (Zondervan), where several other translations make the point even more clear).

Revelation 16:3 makes reference to "every living soul" dying in the sea, using the Greek word "psyche," defined as "animal spirit."

Revelation 4:6-8 describes God's heavenly throne around which "were four beasts full of eyes before and behind," with details reminiscent of Ezekiel 1. They are said to "give glory and honour and thanks to him

103

that sat on the throne, who liveth for ever and ever." Verses 4:6-14 depict the four beasts worshipping Christ the Lamb (also mentioned in 14:3, 5:8 and 11). Were these strange creatures actual, if fantastic, animals living in Heaven, or, as a number of biblical commentators suggest, some kind of angelic beings?

The resurrected Jesus Christ is also depicted in Revelation returning to earth from heaven in the Last Days on a white horse. Although it is not the same as life after death, the prophesied millennial reign of the Messiah, a Judeo-Christian version (which is also described at the end of Revelation includes animals in the picture of a divinely transformed earth in the final phase of history (Isaiah 11:6-9, 65:17-25, Hosea 2:18).

The Bible seems to reflect the preoccupation of its writers with the enormous spiritual and moral problems of humanity. Although scriptures suggesting animal immortality are not very numerous, they do exist, as we have seen. Further, no scripture provides a negative doctrine.

MAINSTREAM CHRISTIANITY

German Protestant reformer Martin Luther (1483-1546) stated that in Heaven or after their resurrection "ants, bugs and all unpleasant stinking creatures will be most delightful and have a wonderful fragrance." Mary Buddemeyer-Porter, in *Will I See Fido in Heaven?* (Companion Press, Box 300, Shippensburg, PA 17257-0310), discusses other indications that Luther accepted the idea all animals were immortal. Yet Lutheran churches today do not take this position.

John Wesley (1703-1791), the founder of Methodism, had this to say: "Something better remains after death of these poor creatures...As a recompense for what they have suffered...they shall enjoy happiness...without alloy, without interruption, and without end...For the Father of All has a tender regard for even his lowest creatures...and will make them large amends for all they suffer..." Yet the Methodist

Church has no official doctrine on whether there are animals in the hereafter to be rendered such justice.

Other Christian leaders, from St. Francis of Assisi to the Rev. Billy Graham, have expressed their personal views on the importance of reverence for life. Popular evangelist Tony Campolo devotes a whole chapter to the "Sacredness of Animals" in his book *20 Hot Potatoes Christians Are Afraid to Touch*.

The International Network for Religion and Animals (Box 1335, North Wales, PA 19454-0335), whose newsletter is edited by a minister for the United Church of Christ, and the Interfaith Council for the Protection of Animals and Nature (4290 Raintree Lane, N.W., Atlanta, GA 30327), which is affiliated with the Humane Society of the United States, have been stimulating interest in animal welfare.

Little, however, has been said by church leaders about the question of animal souls and virtually nothing exists in the way of dogma by any major denomination. It was not always so. As Stanley Cohen documented in the bestseller *The Intelligence of Dogs*, it was only after Augustine that the implications of animals as spiritual beings began to trouble Church leaders. Unlike Luther, they were worried about the appeal of a heaven filled with insects and they also recognized the contradiction of exploiting beings with souls, a preview of the theological debate over African slaves. Philosophers like Rene Descartes (1596-1650) rushed in to support the new doctrine and curry the Church's favor. This led to the scientific attitude that animals were merely biological machines.

As Lew Regenstein points out in *Replenish the Earth*, the Catholic hierarchy has since then made statements about animals that range from denying that they feel pain to urging compassionate treatment. As for the central question here, theologian Carlo Molari expresses the general consensus that "the animal is mortal by definition and so far as we understand now there is no possibility that we will find other creatures in the hereafter." This statement was made to "clarify" a comment by Pope John Paul II in 1989, when he noted the similarity in wording in the Genesis accounts about humans and animals being given the "breath of life," adding that "animals are as near to God as men are," while remaining ambiguous as to what he really meant when he said that "the animals possess a soul." Tom Harpur, a Canadian Catholic and author of *Life After Death* points out that when Genesis says man was formed out of the dust of the ground, it says he "became" a living soul, a combination of spirit and body. This, he argues, means that the animal is a being possessed of energy, thought and personality. They are not made in the image of God, like human beings, but to the extent that they have consciousness, they are souls, too, he believes.

Meantime, as Catholics struggle with their souls over this issue, the international Catholic movement for better treatment of brute creatures is led by the Catholic Study Circle for Animal Welfare (39 Onslow Gardens, South Woodford, London, E18 1ND UK).

Less mainstream churches have tended to either take a negative position on animal survival (Jehovah's Witnesses) or decided that there is no biblical basis for any doctrine on the subject (Seventh-day Adventists). Local churches, especially if they are liberal or mystical, may believe otherwise in the context of an environmentalist theology, but these tend to avoid dogma of any kind.

Vicki Smith engages in biblical research. In a number of discussions with ministers of varying denominations, she found that although most of them did not believe animals have souls, not one of them was able to quote a scripture to support that position. It is sad to hear of grief-stricken individuals who have gone to their minister or priest after the death of a beloved pet only to be told that it has been lost to them forever.

CHRISTIAN SCIENCE

Mary Baker Eddy founded the Church of Christ, Scientist, in 1866, better known as the Christian Scientists. Its primary tenet is that illness and sin are errors of ignorance which can be cured by reading religious texts which will bring one to the understanding that the real world is non-material.

Her basic text, *Science and Health with Key to the Scriptures*, states (p. 514), "All of God's creatures, moving in the harmony of Science, are harmless, useless, indestructible." Later (p. 550) it reads, "God is the Life, or intelligence, which forms and preserves the individual identity of animals as well as of men."

In *Miscellaneous Writings* (p. 36), the question is asked, after a comment that "Mind is immortal," "Do animals and beasts have a mind?" Eddy's answer: "Beasts, as well as men, express Mind as their origin; but they manifest less of Mind...which is God."

THE MORMONS

The most detailed philosophy about animals among significant Christian denominations today can be found in the Church of Jesus Christ of Latter-day Saints, better known as the Mormon church, founded by Joseph Smith in 1830.

One of the first issues addressed by the young church was whether animals possessed spirits, and the answer was that they do (in the Mormon scripture *The Pearl of Great Price*, Moses 3:5, 19). God "created all things...spiritually before they were naturally upon the face of the earth," matching the status of human spirits which are also said to have had an existence in heaven prior to having been born on earth. They would also be resurrected on the millennial earth and in heaven, where they would "enjoy eternal felicity." The four beasts in the Bible's Book of Revelation were actual animals, Smith said it was revealed to him (*Doctrine and Covenants* 77:2-4). "So we see that the Lord intends to save, not only the earth and the heavens, not only man who dwells upon the earth, but all things which he has created," commented Joseph Fielding Smith, one of the church's leading Twelves Apostles at the time and the 10th Prophet of the church in the 1970s. "The animals, the fishes of the sea, the fowls of the air, as well as man, are to be resurrected, or renewed through the resurrection, for they too are living souls," he added.

He and other church leaders were vocal in condemning cruelty to animals and unnecessary killing, warning that all such sins would be paid for at the time of divine judgment. However, many Mormons remain ignorant of these teachings.

EASTERN PHILOSOPHY

Some of the major belief systems which hold that animals have an afterlife are so geographically concentrated that they would not be very relevant to more than a small number of people reading this. Among these would be the animistic religions of Africa, the predominant Japanese religion of Shinto, which holds that all things contain the "kami," or spirits, and two offshoots from Hinduism, Sikhism, whose turbaned adherents believe in reincarnation, and Jainism. The latter has only a few million followers, but it is influential beyond its numbers in India (although constituting less than one percent of the population, the enormously successful Jains—the merchant class of India—provide half the country's taxes). India's animal welfare laws owe much to Jainism, which is indisputably the most compassionate religion in the world. Some Jains even sweep the walk before them to avoid stepping on insects. All of the devout are vegetarians. Jainism regards all souls as sacred and indestructible and ranks them according to the number of senses the religion assigns: gods, humans, and animals are highest with five, shellfish, leeches, worms and similar creatures are at the bottom with two.

Hinduism and Buddhism are the two religions which began in India but became worldwide, with considerable influence in the West. The fundamental problem with discussing them is that after thousands of

108

years of evolution, each has so many sects that it is difficult to generalize about the overall teachings of these religions.

Nominally followed by 80 percent of Indians, Hinduism constitutes a kaleidoscopic religious culture about which one could say almost anything and it would be true, although its philosophers try to mystically reconcile seeming contradictions. The most fundamental division is over the nature of the universe and deity. Classical "impersonal" Hinduism is the form popularized in the West and embraced by New Agers, which says that all things are really one being, *Brahma*, which is pure consciousness, and our separateness is an illusion. From the standpoint of the impersonalist school, the purpose of reincarnation or "samsara," one of the common threads in Hindu philosophy, is to gradually come to realize this delusion through spiritual progress in many lives, and in doing so, begin the process of merging back with the One. Therefore, animals may be former or future human beings, but they are actually non-existent in any ultimate sense, just as we are. That does not preclude a shared, temporary delusion of being with one's pets in a fantasy hereafter or meeting up with a reincarnated spirit on earth again.

Theistic Hinduism, the type most popular in India and best-known here through the Hare Krishna movement, believes that all things are intentional creations of one of the gods, who are themselves creations of Brahman. Individual souls of most living things will continue to exist through endless rebirths, this school teaches. It should be kept in mind, however, that animal's soul here is not conceived as a "pet" with whom one would likely share an afterlife or even coexistent rebirth.

Srila Prabhupada, the founder of Hare Krishna, responded to the question, "How do you know that the animal has a soul?" by noting that animals and humans pursue the same activities, including eating, sleeping, having sex, bearing children, having a living place, and defending themselves. If both are cut they bleed. "Now why do you deny this one similarity, the presence of a soul? That is not logical."

Siddhartha Gautama was a Hindu prince when he started the path which led to his "enlightenment" as the Buddha about 600 B.C. His fundamental insight was that life is suffering due to attachment to the world. Doing the least harm possible to other living things is a Buddhist ideal. But Buddha also taught that there is no soul or even self: rebirth is propelled by attachment to the world and what is reborn is a momentary collection of desires and "karma," the effects of thoughts or deeds which carry the seeds of consequences. No memory or personality survives death in any being, rather, a "drop" or essence continues at least until attachment is extinct, a state indefinable in human terms, labeled "nirvana." What happens after that is a matter of speculation and debate among Buddhists.

Just as similar near-death experiences occur to people of widely varying personal philosophies, those reporting encounters with spirit animals range from fundamentalist Christians to atheists, giving the phenomenon added credibility.

CHAPTER SIX

THE INNER LIVES OF ANIMALS

French philosopher Rene Descartes is most famous for his dictum, "I think, therefore I am." He was asserting that one can only be certain about one's own existence. Animals, if they had any objective existence at all, he claimed, did not think.

He was of the first to articulate the notion, in *Discourse on Method*, that non-human animals had neither intelligence nor any kind of language and were merely biological machines. One of his followers, Nicholas de Malebranche, put Cartesian thinking this way: "Animals eat without pleasure; they cry without pain; grow without knowing it, they fear nothing; they know nothing."

The idea that animals have no intelligence and cannot feel is surely evidence of the proponents' own stupidity. It is obvious to any impartial person who has spent time around animals that they have rich internal lives and communication with them and among them takes place regularly. Stanley Cohen, in *The Intelligence of Dogs*, pointed out that Descartes used faulty logic, propelled by an agenda to deny animals souls.

Jeremy Bentham (1748-1832), an English philosopher, observed that, "A full-grown horse or dog is beyond comparison a more rational, as well as more conversable animal, than an infant of a day or a week or even a month, old. But suppose they were otherwise, what would it avail? The question is not, Can they *reason*? nor Can they *talk*? but, Can they *suffer*?"

We do not think that a human being of subnormal intelligence or mental incapacity should be denied basic rights, yet somehow exploitation of animals is rationalized because they are seemingly not very intelligent.

The immediate and long-lasting effect of Descartes was the institutionalization of his premise in science, which resulted in the use of animals in scientific experiments. Few lay people understand what this really means, but a representative catalogue of what can only be termed torture can be found in Peter Singer's *Animal Liberation*. Although the defense for such experiments is that they are necessary for medical progress, most such claims are demonstrably false, as numerous medical doctors around the world have pointed out in various essays and books (for example, Robert Sharp, M.D., in *The Cruel Deception*, and the newsletters of the Washington, D.C. group, Physicians for Responsible Medicine).

Experimental psychology has been guilty of some of the worst vivisection and psychologists have been fearful of attributing intelligence to animals ever since the Clever Hans, as Stanley Cohen points out. Unfortunately, he and they have the story wrong. Hans was a horse taught by a German schoolteacher at the turn of the century to tap out answers to math problems with his hooves. Psychologists joined the chorus of praise for this wonder horse until it was discovered that he was responding to unintentional cuing, such as an unconscious and barely perceptible nod by his owner when he reached the right number of taps. Everyone knows the story up to that point, and it was this scandal which scared psychologists into being highly suspicious of any claims of animal intelligence.

Scott Rogo researched this story further (see *Psychic Breakthroughs Today*). After Hans' owner died, the horse was passed on to Karl Krall, a wealthy merchant and amateur parapsychologist. Krall designed experiments to eliminate cuing, such as blindfolding, and found that Hans was as clever as ever. Krall was also able to successfully train other horses to answer questions, including one who was blind. He invited some of the best minds in Europe to test them (one was Maurice Maeterlinck, the Belgian Nobel Prize winning author) and the results were impressive.

The extent to which the psychology establishment has a stake in skepticism that animals have an inner life is detailed by Jeffrey Masson, a psychiatrist, and Susan McCarthy, a science writer, in *When Elephants Weep: The Emotional Lives of Animals*. Psychologists' morbid professional fear is of being ridiculed for anthropomorphism, attributing human characteristics to animals. As the authors point out, this aversion has led to highly unscientific, even absurd, positions which are guilty of another intellectual sin, anthropocentricism—seeing things only through human eyes—with our considerable limitations.

In a series of powerful anecdotes, Masson and McCarthy demonstrate what is obvious to most people: many animals show a full range of mental and emotional reactions, including sadness, joy, anger, gratitude and love. They play, they use deception, they show grief and depression when they lose a loved one, they seemingly demonstrate altruism, even across species lines. As Darwin stated in *The Expression of the Emotions in Man and Animals*, the difference between the inner lives of humans and lower animals is one of degree, not kind. If one believes that you can tell how a person is feeling by how they look and behave, it is logical to believe that the same is true of other animals. Even scientists who claim to be agnostic on this treat their pets at home as if the animals' behavior made some sense: the dog seems to be excited about going for a walk, so you take him for one.

We can define intelligence, in part, as the ability to consider choices, to calculate the possible effects of an action, to anticipate what others will do or what they are thinking. Frans de Waal, in *Chimpanzee Politics*, tells the story of a chimp, Luit, at the Arnhem Zoo, whose dominance was challenged by a younger male, Nikkie. De Waal observed Luit as he turned his back on Nikkie and put his hand over his own mouth to hide a nervous grin. When he had finally literally wiped the grin off his face he was able to turn around and act as if nothing had happened. Donald Griffin, professor emeritus of Rockefeller University and author of *Animal Thinking*, believes that such examples of consciousness evolved because mental organization was helpful to survival. As he notes, it is incredibly conceited to assume that humans who have a nervous system like other mammals should have a unique mental life.

Stanley Cohen documents just how wrong our assumption has been that dogs, at least, are not capable of language, both in terms of understanding us and being able to communicate in their own way. In the late 1960s, a number of experiments began to see if primates could engage in real conversations with humans. Koko, a gorilla, learned 600 signs from her trainer, Penny Patterson. The chimpanzee Washoe was taught 170 gestures by Beatrice and Allen Gardner. They were bitterly denounced for being naive and their critics convened conferences to attribute the evidence to trickery, memorized reactions for rewards or the result of cuing. By the 1980s, most animal communication projects had been abandoned.

Some of the trainers started patiently redoing their experiments to make them less vulnerable to criticism. Roger and Debbi Fouts of the University of Central Washington in Ellensburg took over Washoe and began teaching other chimps. Using remote cameras, they found that most "conversations" took place when the trainers were not around (Washoe would sign "hurry" to herself before running to her toilet) and involved play, reassurance or social interaction, rather than being primarily requests for food, as skeptics claimed. And they noticed that the new chimps learned from the others, the first known examples of animals teaching other non-humans a human language (the Foutses even hope to have a colony on a farm to try to teach the chimps agriculture, to see how well they can understand cause and effect). By the mid-

1980s, the respectability of research into the minds of animals had been restored.

One of the most remarkable primate prodigies is Kanzi, a chimpanzee who pushes 250 symbols on a special keyboard which generates spoken English. At his home at the Georgia State University Language Research Center in Atlanta, he is now taught by Sue Savage-Rumbaugh, but he initially learned English by simply observing his trainer's efforts to teach Kanzi's mother (which reminds us that much animal behavior has to be taught to the young by the parents and is therefore not instinctual, as scientists have assumed). Kanzi's particular achievement is his ability to understand grammatical concepts such as syntax (how one can change word order to communicate varying meanings). He even devises his own rules and is considered to have the intelligence of a two-and-a-half-year-old human child.

In one intelligence test, Kanzi watched as a treat was put into a box, which was locked and the key placed inside another box tied by a cord. Kanzi found a piece of flint, hit it against the floor to create a sharp edge, cut the cord and retrieved the key to open the box and get the treat. It is pretty difficult to argue that this is instinct instead of evidence of the ability to think.

Recent studies by Robert Seyfarth and Dorothy Cheney of African vervet monkeys in the wild have shown that they have different cries to communicate warnings about various kinds of predators: a vocabulary, rather than just reactive screeching. Harry Hollien, a University of Florida biologist, has compiled a "tiger dictionary" by playing tape recorded tiger sounds to cats in cages and watching their reactions. Richard Ferraro, a medical electronics expert at the Institute of Applied Physiology and Medicine in Seattle, used a sophisticated device to find out what orcas (killer whales) were communicating. Katherine Payne of Cornell University, who discovered that humpback whale songs change from year to year, found that elephants communicate with sound beyond the range of human hearing. By recording the sound using high-speed tapes and correlating them with what the elephants were doing at the time, she documented their "language."

Jeffrey Masson and Susan McCarthy's *When Elephants Weep* describe the complex social organization this ability to communicate leads to among elephants, who are obviously highly intelligent animals. Among other impressive traits, they will risk their own safety to help other members of the herd, but they have even been known to help out non-elephants in serious trouble.

Perhaps the most intelligent of all mammals, presumably excepting man, are dolphins. Their playfulness and altruism has been noted throughout history. At the Kewalo Basin Marine Mammal Laboratory in Hawaii, Louis Herman directs the training of two female dolphins, Phoenix and Akeakamai, using a modified form of American Sign Language. When instructed to "do something creative together," the dolphins will make up a trick, such as jumping out of the water simultaneously as they spit out jets of water, or swimming backwards, culminating in a synchronized wave of their tails. When they do the right thing, they squeak with pleasure, while a mistake makes them act dejected (or they beat their snouts on the object which "made them wrong").

Diana Reiss of Marineworld/Africa USA in Vallejo, California, has attempted to bridge the communication gap with dolphins by providing them with a submersible keyboard, which they taught themselves to use. It is hooked up to a computer which produces certain sounds for each key and the dolphins have learned to imitate those sounds. "We have to be open to the possibility of true animal consciousness," she says rather conservatively. "Assuming that only humans can give voice to complex thoughts just isn't scientifically sound."

Sea lions are clearly not as intelligent as dolphins, yet Ronald Schusterman has done some eye-opening work with one named Rio at Long Marine Laboratory in Santa Cruz, California. Schusterman taught Rio that a picture of a mug was equivalent to a watch. Then he developed an elaborate procedure to prevent cuing and taught him that if a picture of a dinosaur was equal to the mug, it was also equal to the watch. Rio is shown various pictures to match up and when he is wrong the sea lion barks in frustration. Usually, however, he gets the answer right. What Schusterman's work shows is that an animal does not need to be able to talk or be particularly bright to use reason.

But it is not just mammals who show intelligent characteristics. Theodore Barber's *The Human Nature of Birds* argues that the main reason we have not noticed how like us birds are is because we have not looked very hard. They can exhibit a full range of personality, especially if they are not caged, he notes. "We derisively refer to 'bird brains' because we mistakenly think that there is a necessary correlation between size and intelligence."

The most developed example of a bird personality known is that of a parrot named Alex. Trained for the last 18 years by Irene Pepperberg, professor of ethology (the science of the formation of human character) at Northwestern University, Alex is able to look at a tray of toys and describe, in English, colors, sizes and shapes of various items, including things he has never seen before. When he gets something wrong he says, "I'm sorry," or "I'm gonna go away," before turning his back. When he had to be left overnight at a veterinary hospital for the first time, as Pepperberg was leaving he called out, "Come here. I love you. I'm sorry. Wanna go back."

One of the foremost critics of the experiments of the 1970s was psychologist Herbert Terrace. What changed his mind about animal minds was his work with pigeons, of all things. He trained them to peck colored discs in a particular sequence which became quite lengthy and elaborate. "The only way I could explain their achievement was by attributing certain cognitive skills to them, namely being able to represent a sequence in their minds and keep track of where they are," he says. "Only by turning inward to their own image of the sequence could the pigeons know where they were." The birds also learned to form categories of objects by likeness.

James Gould, a Princeton ethologist, has documented a certain bee behavior which looks to be intelligent. The bee's "waggle dance" is supposed to indicate how the others can locate a source for honey and as he studied it, he hit on an idea to test the insect's ability to "think." Gould would put sugar water near a hive and the bees would go to it to save having to find flowers. Then he would move it further away in a calculated ratio each time. The bees began to anticipate his moves, flying past him to wait at the place where he would be moving it next.

Then there is the story of Sam Rogers, a beekeeper in Myddle, England, who died in 1961. Following the ancient custom of "telling the bees," Rogers' children walked around the hives and announced his death. Later, as relatives gathered around the grave a mile away, a swarm of bees landed on the coffin and stayed there for a half hour before returning to the hives.

The ancient Egyptians, who believed all animals had spirits and who were preoccupied with the afterlife, believed bees to be especially sacred. If that would disturb the Church fathers of the Middle Ages, they would be at least as disturbed about the emerging evidence for mind among ants. As a Discovery Channel documentary on the latest research showed in 1995, they play, build complicated homes, they wage war, they take slaves, they clean each other, they have dozens of signals to communicate, and a complex social organization.

There can be legitimate debate as to how far down the chain of life significant mind extends, but science and society need to finally concede that at least the higher animals can think and feel. Of course, renowned psychics like Beatrice Lydecker and Fred Kimball have been claiming to read animal minds all along, just as shamans among native peoples have always said they routinely "talk" with animals. One psychic specializing in animals, Penelope Smith, is now trying to teach pet owners to read animal minds through seminars, with some demonstrable success (Box

1060, Point Reyes, CA 94956). Most of us know people with such ability to communicate with their companion animals that it seems as if both parties were telepathic. Perhaps this was the secret of the most famous dog trainer of all, Barbara Woodhouse (*No Bad Dogs* and other books), who admitted she was psychic. Her most ardent students could never quite emulate her results.

That we have been blind to the rich internal lives of the animals closest to us, dogs and cats, was revealed to a somewhat startled world by Elizabeth Marshall Thomas in her recent bestsellers, *The Hidden Life of Dogs* and *The Tribe of Tiger*. In a *Newsweek* cover story about the first book, Thomas said she received two questions constantly. One was whether she really allowed her dogs to sleep on her bed. The other was, "Do dogs have souls?" Her answer was, "If we go to heaven, so do they...because if dogs are not there it is not heaven."

But what do intelligence and the ability to feel emotions have to do with the question of whether lower animals are enlivened by spirits in the same manner as most people believe human bodies are? The more we research their inner lives, the more we realize that animals are very much like us. In the case of chimpanzees, this should come as no surprise, since their genetic make-up is only one percent different from ours. If many animals exhibit the full spectrum of personality we have assumed was our preserve, it would be illogical to believe that their inner life is not directed by the type of consciousness we have, which we believe survives death. That is the only conclusion which also matches the anecdotal evidence I have presented in this volume. If it walks like a duck and talks like a duck, it is a duck, we say, so it is only fair that when animal biology and psychology are in significant ways similar to humankind, we should grant these beings the same spiritual nature. When you look into the eyes of a beast, you see the same sparkle of individual personality that you see when you look into the eyes of another human. Perhaps looking out at you is the eternal soul of that being.

We are planning to issue a second volume

in this important subject and would appreciate

hearing from all persons who have had

experiences similar to those recounted in

THE SOUL OF YOUR PET

Please address any experiences, suggestions,

and contributions for the next book to:

Holmes Publishing Group

Attention: Scott S. Smith

Postal Box 623

Edmonds WA 98020